SPEAKER'S SOURCE
BOOK FOR TALKS
TO TEENS

SPEAKER'S SOURCE BOOK FOR TALKS TO TEENS

by

Louis O. Caldwell

BAKER BOOK HOUSE
Grand Rapids, Michigan

Copyright © 1966 by
Baker Book House Company
Reprinted, February, 1972

ISBN: 0-8010-2335-1

Previously printed under the title,
If You Talk to Teens

PHOTOLITHOPRINTED BY CUSHING - MALLOY, INC.
ANN ARBOR, MICHIGAN, UNITED STATES OF AMERICA
1 9 7 2

TO

Rev. Worden McDonald
Who shared a great dream

and

Rev. R. D. Heard
Who issued a great challenge

INTRODUCTION

Today about 11,600 youngsters became teen-agers. They became part of a mushrooming youth population in the middle sixties. Consider the significance of these recent figures given by the United States Department of the Census:

- One out of every two persons in America today is aged twenty-five or under.
- Approximately 27,600,000 of all the youth in our nation are teen-agers.
- This year (1972) 4¼ million teens will become seventeen.
- If the present birth rate continues, by 2020 one out of every three Americans will be aged twenty-five or under.

In the light of this, it becomes obvious that those who do the most to shape the world's future will be youth workers who strike while the iron is hot. According to Bishop Gerald Kennedy, "The world's destiny is being determined by speakers and writers, for better or for worse." This is profoundly true, especially where our youth are concerned.

James S. Stewart rightly called the teen span of life, "God's best chance for a soul." Statistics confirm his point, for more people become Christians at sixteen years of age than any other. Once converted the teen has tremendous potential as a witness for Christ. Billy Graham has asserted that teens are the "greatest evangelists in the world."

This volume has been compiled for the purpose of helping busy youth workers — ministers, teachers, counselors, writers, directors, parents — by making available youth-centered material that has already "worked." It is material I have used in various forms in summer church camps, youth rallies, holiday retreats, youth banquets, training unions, Sunday school and public school classes, devotional meetings in the Houston, Texas, Independent Public School District, and in chapel services at Southern Bible College.

By focusing on the general needs and interests of adolescents, the material used in this volume places emphasis on the "total teen" approach. The successful youth worker keeps in mind the fact that the spiritual, mental, social, emotional and physical aspects of the teen-ager's personality are complex in their interrelatedness, finding expression in a *unity* of being. *All* of the major developmental tasks of youth, therefore, serve as gravitating points of interest for teens. These have helped provide the criteria for the selection and use of the anecdotes, quotes, quips, poems, illustrations, proverbs, statistics, and facts included in these pages.

Scriptural references accompany much of the book's material. This will quickly provide those who give talks of a devotional nature with the essence of relatively short addresses.

The book is indexed by Scripture, Names and Subjects. This, with the Table of Contents, provides the user with four handy ways of finding desired material.

Very few applications of the material are explicitly drawn. This frees the material from being unnecessarily limited. Speakers with insight and ingenuity will find that the same anecdote, for example, can be used effectively in many ways. Humor is apparent throughout the volume and should protect the user of the book from suffering the consequences of the "frowning saint" presentation. Speakers as well as writers can profit by C. H. Spurgeon's remark: "There is no particular virtue in being seriously unreadable."

No copyrighted material has been intentionally used without written permission, which has been gratefully acknowledged under the material quoted. To trace the source of all that has been included is impossible. However, any oversight brought to my attention will be corrected if other printings are called for.

A great debt of gratitude is owed to Dr. Esther Marion Nelson, professor emeritus of the University of Houston, and Professor Grady Manley of Southern Bible College. It was in Dr. Nelson's class that I first became impressed by the need and advantage of orderly, systematic filing. Professor Manley was responsible for introducing me to a "system." Without these two influences, this book would still be scattered throughout my study in boxes, drawers and folders!

Special thanks go to the many contributors of useful material and references and to the several persons who typed and corrected the manuscript: Mrs. Sally Clark, Mrs. Carolyn Anderwald, Miss Betty Nichols, Miss Kay Kasai, Miss Harlena Thomas, Miss Nellie Gobbard, Miss Sandra Redmon and Mr. J. B. Williams.

This is my fourth book by Baker Book House and, like the first three, it has received the discerning attention of the editor, Mr. Cornelius Zylstra. His suggestions and guidance are gratefully acknowledged.

Louis O. Caldwell

Southern Bible College
Houston, Texas

TABLE OF CONTENTS

Introduction 7

I. Developing A Healthy Self-image 11

II. Achieving A Responsible Role In The Family . . 32

III. Expanding Mental Horizons 51

IV. Building More Mature Friendships 74

V. Relating To God In Christ 94

VI. Planning For The Future 120

VII. Indexes 141

DEVELOPING A HEALTHY

SELF-IMAGE

1. Ps. 17:5; 19:12; Prov. 4:7, 8

When I was born, my mother sighed,
"I'm glad my baby is blue-eyed
And that he has blond curly hair
And a complexion that is fair."
My father looked at me and said
"He has a fine, well-rounded head —
He'll be a whiz at the 3 R's."
And then he passed out big cigars.
But soon things seemed to go awry.
"All that child does is wet and cry,"
My mother wailed, and I could see
She had my father's sympathy.
At one, they said, "He'll never walk."
At two, they said, "He'll never talk."
At three, they said, "He talks all day!"
At four, "He's always in the way!"
And then my childhood days were spent
In hearing parental lament
About the naughty things I did
And how I'd be a "problem kid."
It seems that I made "too much noise"
And that I played with "the wrong boys."
I got "too dirty, ruined my clothes,"
And wore my shoes out "at the toes."
At mealtimes I was "always late,"
I "swang upon the backyard gate,"
In fact, whatever I thought fun
Was "something that should not be done."
Now I'm a teen-ager, and boy!
Those childhood days were days of joy
Compared with what I go through now!
It seems we're always in a row
About the car, the girls I date,
And because I stay out late,
And talk too long upon the phone,

And want some money of my own.
The only thing at which I'm good
Is in being misunderstood.

— John M. Gran, *How to Understand and Teach Teen-Agers,*
T. S. Denison and Company, pp. 65, 66 (used by permission)

2. The Teen-Age Tidal Wave

This is the year America's postwar baby boom began to come home to roost, says the Population Reference Bureau. The bureau has the figures to prove it.

The number of teen-agers celebrating their seventeenth birthday in 1964 is 3,700,000 — a fantastic one million zoom over the 1963 crop.

These youngsters were born in 1947, back in the days when the slogan "Boom Babies Mean Boom Business" was popular. At that time, there were only forty-three million Americans aged seventeen and under; today there are seventy million.

Today these boom babies constitute not only the nation's greatest resource but the greatest social challenge facing this country which, despite its prosperity can't seem to budge unemployment below a constant 5 per cent mark. Consider these statistics:

°One-fourth of these 3.7 million teen-agers have already dropped out of school. Most of them are adrift on a labor market that has less need for unskilled labor.

°One-third of the boys will be rejected for military service when they are examined after their eighteenth birthday, mostly because of educational deficiencies.

°Twelve per cent of the girls and 2 per cent of the boys are already married. (A fifth of these girls are destined to be divorced or separated; one out of every three seventeen-year-old husbands will be.)

Each new crop of seventeen-year-olds will be larger than the last, leveling off at about four million. Over the next quarter-century, the number of women in their peak childbearing years will be doubled. Despite a decline in the birth rate after 1947, this broader population base inevitably will mean a repetition of the baby boom.

In absolute numbers, the Population Reference Bureau estimates that 6.5 million new babies will be arriving annually by 1980. If the trend continues, the nation's population will pass 360 million by the year 2000 and a billion by 2065.

When that notable day dawns, every other American will be a teen-ager.

—From an Editorial in the *Bryan Eagle*

3. At the time the Declaration of Independence was signed, over half the nation was under eighteen.

4. Strange Things (Isa. 5:12; Luke 5:26)

> As I was going out one day
> My head fell off and rolled away,
> But when I saw that it was gone,
> I picked it up and put it on.

> When I got into the street
> A fellow cried, "Where are your feet?"
> I looked at them and sadly said,
> "I've left them both asleep in bed!"

5. Of the twenty-two and one-half million teens in this country, no two will grow in the same way. Growth is determined by four important glands: the thyroid, pituitary, thymus, and sex glands. Normal growth occurs when these four glands operate normally and have the proper balance.

Some other remarkable facts about rapid teen growth are:

1. The size of the heart doubles during the teens. Many young people damage their hearts by over-exerting themselves. To avoid this, get plenty of rest, along with good regular exercise. (The *other* kind of heart trouble is not so simple to avoid!)

2. Body weight increases twelve pounds per year on the average.

3. Girls outgrow boys until the mid-teens (15 or 16). Then they catch up to and pass them — to the delight of both sexes!

4. Teens eat 20 per cent more food than adults.

5. Teen-agers gulp down 3½ billion quarts of milk every year.

6. Teens use over seven hundred muscles and seven million brain cells daily. (Ps. 100:3; Eph. 2:10)

6. Alcohol; Drinking (an enemy of growth) (Prov. 23:29, 30; Isa. 24:9; Eph. 5:18)

1. Seventy per cent of all chronic alcoholics began drinking as teen-agers.

2. One in every nine social drinkers becomes an alcoholic.

3. A jigger of whiskey, an average 3½ ounce glass of wine, and a bottle of beer all contain about the same amount of alcohol.

4. One drink, on the average, will have an effect on your judgment (defined in dictionary as "good sense") and inhibitions (inner force that restrains natural acts).

5. Alcohol affects vision, speech, and balance — and in time your consciousness.

6. Drinking drivers cause twenty thousand deaths a year.

7. Enough alcohol can kill you.

As Dr. Joseph Molner, writing in *The Houston Post,* said, "Taking one [drink] without disaster doesn't mean that you can take another, for drinking *can* become a habit.

"Too many families know the result of sliding into the habit.

"Too many young people don't know."

7. What Smoking Can Do for You (Rom. 12:1; Heb 12:1)

1. It will disqualify you for sports. No good coach will allow his players to smoke, because he knows that smoking makes you short-winded. No one can smoke and be in top physical condition.

2. Smoking will discolor your teeth and fingers. Your smile tells people a lot about you, and so do cigarette stains.

3. Your breath and clothes will smell unpleasant to those who do not smoke.

4. Smoking may provide you with lung cancer. Daniel Horn of the Cancer Research Society warns: "We have found out that smoking cigarettes causes lung cancer. We did not use to know this."

5. You will not do as well in school. Donald K. Pumroy, a psychologist, has said that cigarette smoking students do not make as good grades on the average as non-smokers. His studies point out that the more a student smokes, the lower his grades are likely to be.

6. You will be deprived of thousands of dollars in a lifetime, if you smoke. Let's do some figuring:

If $0.35 — Average price of a package of cigarettes

and   7 — Number of packs smoked in a week (this is a minimum)

$2.45 — Cost per week

then   4.3 — Number of weeks in a month

735

980

$10.535 — Cost per month

12 — Number of months in a year

$210.70

10535

$126.42 — Cost per year

50 — Number of years average person smokes

$6,321.00 — Enough money to buy one of the most expensive cars on the market!

14

8. A Study of Smoking Habits among Seventh to Twelfth Graders in Newton, Massachusetts, showed:

Non-smokers seem not only to be of higher social and economic groups; they are also better students.

The non-smokers achieve much better than smokers — especially than heavy smokers.

Non-smokers tend to read more books and belong to more organizations.

Smokers watched more television, went to more movies and owned more cars.

The heavier a smoker the student was, the less likely he was to believe that smoking was harmful.

Teen-agers who smoked usually belonged to crowds of others who smoked.

Smokers seem to have fewer inner resources than non-smokers.

When the smokers were asked why they had begun and were continuing to smoke, they often gave such answers as, "I want to be part of the crowd," or "I don't want to be an oddball."

They seemed to be more interested in impressing others and in appearing to be adult than the non-smokers did.

—Dr. Eva Salber, Harvard University

9. "For both youth and adults the habitual use of cigarettes is incompatible with the biblical principle of the stewardship of the body. For Christian adults in particular, it contributes by force of example to teen-age addiction to a dangerous and often fatal habit and thus violates the biblical principle of responsibility for one's brother. No longer may it be considered a harmless, optional practice to be taken up merely for personal gratification."

— Editorial, *Christianity Today*,
No. 8, 1963

10. The VD Menace (Micah 6:7; Gal. 6:7)

Nation-wide, the number of reported new cases of syphilis rose from fifty-six hundred in 1957 to twenty thousand in 1962.

Among teen-agers the incidence has increased 200 per cent since 1957.

Much of this increase has been among the upper socio-economic group.

Taxpayers are paying $50 million annually to care for the syphilitic insane. They're paying another $6 million to care for those blinded by syphilis.

— From an interview with William F. Schwartz, Consultant for the VD branch, Communicable Diseases Center, U.S. Public Health Service

11. Dear Adam and Eve (Num. 1:8; Ps. 16:6; Titus 3:9)

Three monkeys, dining in a coconut tree
   Were discussing something they thought shouldn't be;
Said one to the others: "Now listen, you two
   Here's something that cannot be true —
That humans descended from our noble race!
   What, it's a shock, a terrible disgrace!
Whoever heard of a monkey deserting his wife
   Or leaving a baby and ruining its life?
I've never known a monkey so selfish to be
   As to build a fence 'round a coconut tree
So that other monks couldn't get even a taste
   While bushels of coconuts were going to waste.
And here's another thing us monkeys won't do —
   Carouse, make whoopee and disgrace our lives
Then swing on home and beat up our wives.
   Yes, those humans think it's great to fuss and cuss;
They're descended from *something*, but it can't be us!"

—Anonymous

12. The atoms in the body have an energy potential of 11,400,000 kwh per pound. Evaluated in dollars, the value of every pound is $570,000,000!

13. Teens may grow as much as six inches in one year. Growth continues to twenty-five years of age. Maximum height is reached by age thirty-five, then shrinkage begins to occur — about four-tenths of an inch every ten years. This is due to the drying of the cartilage in the joints of the spinal column. (Isa. 9:2)

14. Growing pains are caused by bones growing faster than muscles. Awkwardness is due to the muscles outgrowing the bones.

15. Mental Health (Ps. 42:11)

"Physical symptoms often stem from man's depressed feeling. For forty years I have been saddened to see that commonly when a person goes into a mental depression (melancholia) we doctors fail to make the correct diagnosis.

"One of the common symptoms of melancholia is abdominal pain. Usually the patient talks of great fatigue. Many have insomnia . . . lose their appetites . . . feel strange and 'not themselves' . . . have headaches and . . . so much pain about their joints they are thought to have arthritis.

"If questioned closely, they may admit that they feel terribly unhappy. . . . At least a third of the people who came to me with some serious disease in the abdomen turned out to have their trouble in the brain!"

—Dr. Walter C. Alvarez, *Grit*

16. Usefulness

> The chap who split the atom
> Rates no halo or hozanna
> Like the soda fountain phizzisist
> Who split the first banana!

17. True beauty works from the inside and radiates from a heart in which Christ dwells. "Heavenly cosmetics" cannot be put on, but can be prayed in and lived out. (Ps. 90:17; Isa. 52:7; I Peter 3:4)

18. Facts about Hair (Matt. 10:30)

One thousand per square inch of scalp, varying with age and color.

Average person has about 110,000 hairs on scalp.
Blonde — 160,000
Brunette — 110,000
Redhead — 50,000

Normal adult has 120 square inches of scalp area that in seventy years will grow 240 ounces. If not cut, in seventy years hair would be 35 feet long. (Judg. 16:17; Ps. 40:12; Matt. 10:30)

19. Short men have cast long shadows. Jonathan Edwards, who stood 5 feet 6 inches, was said to have had the greatest mind in the ranks of the ministry in his generation. Charles Spurgeon, no taller than Edwards, was preaching to crowds numbering in the thousands by the time he was twenty. James Madison, our fourth president, stood 5 feet 4 inches. (Isa. 16:7)

20. Christ's biography in the four Gospels has nothing to say about His height and weight. His life, not His size, is what mattered to the inspired writers.

21. Nutritionist Flays Diet of Teen-agers (II Sam. 20:9)

Washington (UPI) — A health equation for today's youth: A poor diet, plus a heavy social schedule, minus regular meals, equals one poorly fed teen-ager.

This was the essence of a statement Friday by an Agriculture Department nutritionist, who contended America's teen-aged girls and boys are probably the worst-fed members of their families.

The problem is not that there isn't enough quantity to the food, but the quality leaves something to be desired from a nutrition standpoint, Dr. Evelyn Spindler said.

Teen-age girls seem to have more problems with their diets, Dr. Spindler said, mainly because they are girls. For example:
- They fear getting fat.
- They spend extra time dressing. This increases their chance of skipping breakfast to make a bus to school.

• Dinner may be skipped if it interferes with a date.

"Six out of every ten girls and four out of every ten boys have poor diets," Dr. Spindler said.

Research shows the older the child the poorer the diet, she declared and also criticized the ability of the teen-ager to pick his own food.

Most teen-age diets, Dr. Spindler said, are low in iron. Foods that are high in sugar and fat often replace those with the much needed protein, minerals and vitamins.

The real effect of the bad diets tends to show up when teen-age girls marry, the nutritionist emphasized.

According to Dr. Spindler, "Babies born to undernourished teen-agers may be premature, have congenital defects, or lack adequate nutritional reserves to protect them through birth and the first few months of life. Undernourishment during pregnancy may leave a permanent mark on the young mother."

Said Dr. Spindler: There is nothing wrong with a teen-ager eating a hamburger or a piece of pizza, if he eats a green salad, a banana and a milkshake along with it. As unappetizing as this type of meal may sound, it is better than a combination of a soft drink and potato chips.

— Robert Buckhorn, *Houston Chronicle,*
May 22, 1965

22. To stay young, associate with young people. To get old in a hurry, try keeping up with them.

23. A father noted that his teen-age daughter had entered an awkward age — she knows how to make a phone call, but not how to end one.

24. Changing times: The perfect gift for an eighteen-year-old used to be a compact. It still is — if it has four wheels.

25. The worst thing about the younger generation is that a lot of us don't belong to it anymore.

26. Adolescence is that time in a boy's life when he notices that a girl notices he is noticing her.

27. Middle age is when the narrow waist and the broad mind begin to change places.   —*Fort Nelson* (Canada) *News*

28. An adult has been defined as a person who has stopped growing at both ends and started growing in the middle.

29. He who thinks himself green will grow; who thinks himself ripe will rot.

30. Eccles. 5:12; Luke 6:24; 12:33

When billionaire J. Paul Getty was asked why he didn't retire and cash in all his possessions, he said, "If I sold everything, where would I put the money?"

Now this would be quite a problem.

You learn in school that the government only insures deposits up to $10,000 each. This would mean that one hundred thousand banks would be needed to take care of a billion dollars.

Think of the time this would take! If he opened a $10,000 account every hour, eight hours a day, forty hours a week, it would take him forty-eight years to deposit all that money.

This would involve another problem. Each new account would include the receiving of a deposit book. And what to do with one hundred thousand deposit books? At, say, half an ounce a piece, those little deposit books would require a 1½ ton truck just to be hauled around!

> — An adaptation from an article in a metropolitan newspaper in Dallas, Texas, by Jack Guinn

31. The official yell of the School of Experience is "Ouch."
—Times, Crisfield, Missouri

32. If you lose confidence in yourself that makes the vote unanimous.

33. Dieting: The penalty for exceeding the feed limit.

34. Diets are recommended for those who are thick and tired of it.

35. More people commit suicide with a fork than any other weapon.

36. Doctors have discovered that a merry person resists disease better than a sour puss.   —Roger Allen

37. With coarse food to eat, water to drink, and the bended arm for a pillow, happiness may still exist.   —Chinese Proverb

38. A teen-ager is an "it" growing into a he or she.

39.   Life is hard by the yard,
                     By the inch it's a cinch.

40. Ps. 19:10; Prov. 28:10

U.S. teen-age boy's income is $10.00 a week, one-third of which is earned through part-time work and summer jobs.

Here's how it's spent:

$2.30	school lunches
1.00	dating
.90	snacks
.90	entertainment, records, etc.
.70	clothes
.70	savings
.60	school supplies
.50	reading magazines
.40	cars and gas
1.10	sports
.30	hobbies
.20	grooming
.40	miscellaneous

41. Work is the yeast that raises the dough. — *The Irish Digest*

42. Rom. 12:1; I Cor. 11:20-33; 15:3

San Francisco (UPI) — Leonole Modell, the girl who swam the length of Lake Tahoe at the age of thirteen, the English Channel at fourteen and now plans to become the first woman to swim the channel round-trip, believes in "cool" training.

Before each dip she takes a one-hour bath in a tub filled with ice cubes.

"I don't mind," she says, "if there is a TV nearby."

43. Ps. 74:16; Matt. 6:34; James 5:11

Dr. Marshall Lund, the great orthopedic surgeon, had as a patient a girl who was taller than most men. Her height was reduced by surgery. When she asked, "Doctor, how long will I have to lie here?" the surgeon cheerfully answered: "Only one day at a time."

44. Girls the Weaker Sex

An embarrassing picture of American youth appeared recently, when a test of physical fitness was given to eighty-five hundred American and ten thousand British young people.

The only victory for America was in ball-throwing. It was found that in all other tests British boys were far superior to American boys, and that in certain tests British girls were superior to American boys!

45. Mistaken Values (Job 28:16; Phil. 3:7)
> To get his wealth
> He spent his health,
> And then with might and main,
> He turned around and spent his wealth
> To get his health again.

46. Gen. 1:26, 27; III John 1:2
> He who formed our frame
> Made man a perfect whole,
> And made the body's health
> Depend upon the soul.
>> — Anonymous

47. Teen-ager in shoe store to friend: "It's a difficult choice — I need a pair that will bring me to Roger's shoulder, but not over Herbie's head."

48. The only exercise some folks get is jumping to conclusions, running down their friends, sidestepping responsibility, and pushing their luck.

49. "Fearfully and Wonderfully Made"
What a piece of work is man! How noble in reason! How infinite in faculty! In form and moving how express and admirable! In action how like an angel! In apprehension how like a god! The beauty of the world! The paragon of animals!
>> —From Shakespeare's *Hamlet*

50. A Movie Director's Statement to an Actress:
"Just remember, never forget that all you are is a piece of meat, like in a butcher shop."

51. Isa. 26:21; Prov. 12:15; Rom. 16:18
> Mary had a little lamb
> A lobster and some prunes,
> A glass of milk, a piece of pie,
> And then some macaroons;
> It made the naughty waiters grin
> To see her order so;
> And when they carried Mary out,
> Her face was white as snow.

52. Teen-age Inventors (Acts 3:6; I Cor. 7:7)
Men of mature years cannot claim to have made all the contributions to world progress. Teen-aged inventors and scientists

have written the following headlines along the road to our more advanced civilization:

1581 — Seventeen-year-old Galileo startles the scientific world with a treatise on the pendulum, written while a student at the University of Pisa in Italy. He admits making some of his experiments atop the celebrated Leaning Tower of Pisa, the first time that structure has been put to any practical use.

1751 — Fifteen-year-old James Watt becomes curious about the steaming teakettle in the kitchen of his mother's house at Greenock, Scotland. "All that steam power shouldn't be going to waste," declared thrifty Jimmie. "If it could be harnessed, I might perfect a steam engine and become famous!"

1787 — Twelve-year-old Alexander Anderson begins engraving on copper and type method in New York City. "No one instructed me how to do it," admits Alex. "I just picked it up from watching jewelers at work."

1827 — Eighteen-year-old Cyrus Hall McCormick experiments with an idea for speeding up the harvesting of America's grain crops. Within a half-dozen youthful years he expects to patent his reaping machine. It will be hailed as one of the greatest advances in scientific farming and a boon to the economic life of the world.

1859 — Twelve-year-old Thomas Alva Edison learns to operate the telegraph instrument while working for the Grand Trunk Railroad on the run between Detroit and Port Huron.

1861 — Fifteen-year-old George Westinghouse designs a rotary engine while working in his father's machine shop at Schenectady, New York. Young George boasts that some day he will invent a safety device for stopping railroad trains — with compressed air.

1864 — Seventeen-year-old Thomas Alva Edison has just taken out a patent on an automatic telegraph repeater. This is just the first of a promised twelve hundred patents to be secured in what looks like a busy lifetime ahead of Tom Edison.

—*Sunshine*

53. The Punctuation Marks of Youth (Luke 2:20)

The period. Your teens mark the end of your childhood. People no longer look upon you as a child. Childish actions are to be put away. You are wading out into the waters of a new life, and there's no turning back! Accept the challenge of your teens and, as Paul said to his spiritual son, Timothy, "Let no man despise thy youth; but be thou an example of the believers, in the word, in conversation, in charity [love], in spirit, in faith, in purity" (I Tim. 4:12).

The comma. Your teens are a *pause* between childhood and

adulthood. Growing up may seem as if it will take a lifetime to you. But any adult will tell you that this period of your life is like a strawberry Coke in the hands of a thirsty teen-ager — it doesn't last very long!

The Exclamation Point. This is an *exciting* time of your life. Many "firsts" crowd your teens with thrills. Your first date, your first pair of high heels, your solo drive in the family car, and many other new activities fill your life with excitement.

The Question Mark. The adolescent years are years of *uncertainty.* You have more question marks in your mind than you see in your text books. "What do people think about me? Will I be a success? What will my husband or wife look like — if I ever get married? What about God? . . . heaven? . . . hell?" These and many other questions put you in occasional, thoughtful moods. No wonder the poet wrote:

The thoughts of youth are long, long thoughts.

— From *It's Great To Be YOUng,*
by the author

54. Contentment

I wish I were a fish in a way
'Cause all they do is swim and play:
No tests to take, no bills to pay —
But I had a trout for dinner today!
— Louis O. Caldwell

55. Action

I am only one,
But still I am one;
I cannot do everything,
But still I can do something;
And because I can not do everything,
I will not refuse to do the something
That I can do.
— Edward Everett Hale

56. Teen Commandments (Prov. 12:15; Isa. 1:18)
1. Resist temptation.
2. Overcome despondency.
3. Maintain your confidence.
4. Grow spiritually.
5. Have a *definite* prayer time.
6. Read your Bible *regularly.*
7. Have some personal convictions.
8. Pray for a vision and a burden.
9. Witness for Christ each day.
10. Show courage at all times.

— Clipped

57. How To Be Perfectly Miserable (Esther 3:1-6)
1. Think about yourself.
2. Talk about yourself.
3. Use "I" as often as possible.
4. Mirror yourself continually in the opinion of others.
5. Listen greedily to what people say about you.
6. Expect to be appreciated.
7. Be suspicious.
8. Be jealous and envious.
9. Be sensitive to slights.
10. Never forgive a criticism.
11. Trust nobody but yourself.
12. Insist on consideration and respect.
13. Demand agreement with your own views on everything.
14. Sulk if people are not grateful to you for favors shown them.
15. Never forget a service you have rendered.
16. Be on the lookout for a good time for yourself.
17. Shirk your duties if you can.
18. Do as little as possible for others.
19. Love yourself supremely.
20. Be selfish.

— Clipped

58. Sometimes You Just Can't Win

Three Russian teen-age boys were sitting in a Russian prison. They were talking of what they were accused of:

The first said: I was three minutes late and they accused me of giving information to American spies.

The second said: I was five minutes early and they accused me of learning facts to give to American spies.

The third said: I was right on time and they accused me of having an American watch.

—Contributed by a student

59. Overcoming Difficulty

A little brown cork
Fell in the path of a whale
Who lashed it down
With its angry tail.
But, in spite of the blows,
It quickly arose,
And floated serenely
Before his nose.
Said the cork to the whale,
"You may flap and sputter and frown,
But you never, never can keep me down.

For I'm made of stuff
That is buoyant enough
To float instead of to drown."

— Anonymous

60. It's not the size of the dog in the fight, but the size of the fight in the dog that counts.

61. The Tormented Generation (Jer. 15:18; Rom. 2:9; II Cor. 1:3, 4)

* The scene is a respected eastern men's college; the time is night. A young man, wildly drunk and loudly profane, is walking along a ledge on the fourth floor of his dormitory while police, doctors and friends hold their breath below.

* The scene is a large university in the West; the time is two a.m. A young girl slips softly out of her sorority house and hurries to a car in which a frightened young man is waiting to drive her to an abortionist in a city a hundred miles away.

* The scene is a railroad track not far outside Philadelphia; the time is early morning. An onrushing train screeches to stop, but not before its wheels have decapitated an eighteen-year-old coed, who, a minute earlier, had calmly lain down with her neck on the rail.

Many college students find college a time of confusing misery, frustration and failure. This is revealed by the following statistics:

1. 20 per cent of students at the University of Pennsylvania require help from mental-health service during their college years.
2. 25 per cent of Harvard's undergraduates consult a psychiatrist or social worker.
3. 15 per cent of the students from institutions seek psychiatric help — while 30 per cent ought to.

Variety of forms emotional distress takes:

1. headaches	2. nightmares	3. cramps or retching before examinations
4. fatigue	5. overweight	6. forgetfulness

These were observed by campus physicians and nurses.

Common causes of student deaths:

1. Nationally, suicide is the sixth most common cause.
2. Accidents first at Yale.
3. Suicide second at Yale.

It would be comforting to discover a single cause for the emotional troubles that afflict nearly a third of our college students.

Some of the students' pressures are put on them by their parents. Some of these are: excessive emphasis on academic success in college; and dictation of their choice of career.

Not all the pressures are put on the students by their parents. One student said, "We tell each other again and again how many of us are likely to flunk out, and we pass on all the rumors about how only the top guys get decent jobs. We work ourselves into a real lather and grind away at our books all night. No wonder we get stomach trouble or nightmares."

Moreover, the increased academic competition harms not only the less capable students but many of the extremely bright ones as well.

Many who were outstanding in their local public school were shocked and depressed that with so much competition they do not do as well.

Several things may result from this:
1. Many may lack the self-discipline to raise their grades, and let themselves slide into a discard heap.
2. Others furiously goad themselves on in a single-minded dedication that, at the very least, makes their lives miserable and may lead to more serious trouble.

Dean James H. Robertson of the University of Michigan says that the chief cause for this is "personal unreadiness or immaturity." People with a personality disorder are often irresponsible, impulsive and lacking in conscience; they do what they please without caring what society will think of them.

Another factor contributing to tension on the campus is the universal problem of growing up, which psychoanalyst Erik Erikson has called "the identity crisis." There are two main aspects of the collegian's identity crisis.
1. Choice of career
2. Sex

"Am I really a man?" is a painful question for any youth — particularly when he can answer it only by attempts at seduction or early marriage.

Sex is a somewhat different problem with the girl. She wants to prove her desirability, but she is well aware that the premarital sex is not sanctioned by her parents, her church, her school, or even many of her friends. In several recent surveys the majority of college women admit that at times they have "gone further" than they should have, and that they feel guilty about it.

Another problem is the great influx of students. At the larger state colleges and universities school populations are so huge — total enrollments of fifteen to twenty thousand are becoming commonplace — that students are apt to feel lost and ignored. Some exist as virtual nonentities, wretchedly lonely for four years. Others make frantic efforts to become known on campus.

Parents should also consider ways of reducing the shock of a late-maturing child's first plunge into college life. Instead of going out of town his first year, he could go to a school in the vicinity of his home — and plan to transfer elsewhere his second or even third year.

Our sons and daughters may not be able to echo the words of the Yale graduate of 1928, who said as he strolled through the court of his former dormitory, "I can recall only one unhappy period when I was here. That was in May of my senior year, when I suddenly thought, 'It's nearly over — the best time of my life!'" But neither need they reflect the sentiments of the bitter senior at M.I.T. who recently said, "It's a rat race, a grind, a meaningless ride on a roller coaster. I'm just counting the days till it's over."

> — Compiled by Morton M. Hunt and Rena Corman
> *Saturday Evening Post,* October 12, 1963
> Condensed by Martha Moore

62. Teens from fourteen to seventeen spend $18 million a year.

63. An estimated 11,065,000 teen-age girls across the nation spend $6.3 billion a year. More than nine million boys spend $16 billion.

64. Teen population and buying power are on the increase. This year 3,100,000 teens will celebrate their seventeenth birthday. Ten years from now four million will reach seventeen.

65. Eleven million teen-age girls spend $321 million a year to buy 56 per cent of all the records and record albums in the country. Boy and girl teen-agers now spend $10 billion annually. By 1970 the amount will jump to $21 billion.

> — Condensed from *Parade,* October 11, 1964

66. By 1965 half the people in the United States will be under twenty-five years of age, constituting the fastest-growing segment in the consumer market. Some twelve million of these girls from fifteen to twenty-four years old will spend $5 million a year on clothes, average of $430 apiece.

67. When some people are given responsibility, they grow; others merely swell.

68. The first symptom of helplessness is the dodging of responsibility, the effort to unload on somebody else.

69. Honor

"To have a sense of honor is to be grown-up, not necessarily to be over 21 years of age, or even to be of 12 — but grown-up in the sense of being worthy of trust. Honor is something that each individual should be proud of. Even if the world doesn't know your good deed, just for yourself to know, and have a clear conscience, that you have done the right thing is rewarding within itself."

— Sharon Ford, American Legion Award Winner

70. Very early, I perceived that the object of life is to grow.
— Margaret Fuller

71. Failure is only the opportunity to begin again, more intelligently.
— Henry Ford

72. Formula for failure: Try to please everyone.
— Herbert Bayard Swope

73. Failure is the line of least persistence. — Stephanic Marting

74. Teacher: "What happens to little girls who don't eat their meals?"
Male Student: "They grow up to be fashion models. . . ."

75. Teen-ager writing home from boarding school: "Send food packages! All they serve here is breakfast, lunch, and dinner."

76. You can only stay a teen-ager seven years, but you can stay immature indefinitely.

77. A second rate *something* is better than a first rate *nothing!*

78. Every time a boy goes bad, a good man dies.

79. The very best angle to approach any problem is from the try angle!

80. The largest room in the world is the room for improvement.

81. The man of the hour is usually one who made every minute count.

82. A character is greater than a career.

83. We see things not as they are, but as we are.

84. Everyone is a moon, and has a dark side which he never shows to anyone.   —Mark Twain

85. Problems can be used as steppingstones instead of stumblingblocks. For it's not how big your problems are, but how big you are that makes the difference.

86.   My strength is as the strength of ten
              Because my heart is pure.

87. Never try to leap over a chasm in two jumps.

88. Britain's 5½ million teens spend one billion pounds ($2,800,-100,000) per year more than it takes to run the British Army and Navy.

89. Life will grind you down or polish you up — it depends on what kind of material you are made of.

90. It takes ten years to grow an oak; six months to grow a squash.

91. Too far east is west.

92. God gives birds their food — but they must fly for it.

93. When I go to bed, I leave my troubles in my clothes.

94. Teen Slang:
Flakey means bad.
A clod is a person you don't like.
Spastic is something odd or different.
Fern docks means anything you want it to mean.

95. One-third of all eighteen-year-olds registering for selective service are physically or mentally unfit.

96. Negativism (Job 37:21)
Most people who are born with or acquire a handicap let it get them down.

They waste years of their lives getting pickled in the vinegar of their own depression. They develop an introverted and sour personality. Disgruntled, irascible, disappointed, they become envious and irritable, constantly bemoan the unkind fate which made them too tall, too short, not pretty or handsome or rich enough.   — Lloyd Shearer

97. Attitude

Don't let your attitudes harden; this can be more fatal than hardening of the arteries.

Keep your capacity for wonder.
Keep on being creative.
Keep trying new things.
Develop a workable philosophy of life.

— War Cry

98.   Many a genius has been slow of growth.
Oaks that flourish for a thousand years
Do not spring up into beauty like a reed.
— George Henry Lewis

99. The mighty oak began with the tiny acorn.

100. The eye can be trained. Some eyes see only roses; some only thorns. What do you look for in the circumstances of your life?   *— Hi Call*

101. Being young is a fault which nature improves one day at a time.

102. Past experience should be a guide post, not a hitching post.

103. The Christian Athlete (Ps. 31:3; John 10:27)

On the antique-designed letter sheet of the Fellowship of Christian Athletes, a national institution, is emblazoned this bit of heart-warming appeal:

And, Dear God,
If older folks were once like me,
And dreamed the dreams that I now see,
Would you ask them if they might show
A younger fella that right way to grow?

104. The Best Years (Ps. 71:1)

Were you ever a Teen-ager?
What did you see? What did you feel?
Were you ever by the sea at dusk,
Have you ever heard the crying of the waves
As they break against the rocks,
Seen the Moonlight set the sea ablaze,
Felt the moon beams were a staircase
On which to walk out over the waters
And keep right on up to the sky?
I did, and then I would cry.

I don't know why.
Does life seem so complex?
One minute you laugh
Till your sides ache.
And next you're crying
Because your heart aches.
And all the while you wonder why.
Is it possible to be so very sure
That you know you could make no mistake,
And at the same time be so uncertain
You think your head will surely break
From all this confusion?

—Eileen Madden
 Catherine McAuley High School
 Brooklyn, New York
 American Red Cross Journal, January, 1966

ACHIEVING A RESPONSIBLE
ROLE IN THE FAMILY

105. J. Edgar Hoover Advises Parents (Prov. 22:6; Luke 2:51)

How to Raise a Delinquent

"What can I do to keep my boy out of trouble?"

No one at Boys' Clubs has the whole answer to such a basic question. But there are some definite clues, gained through a century of working with boys. For example, Boys' Clubs can almost guarantee that your boy will get into trouble *if:*

• He gets whatever he asks for, because it's easier than arguing.

• You pride yourself on not prying into his life — where he spends his time, his friends, his after school activities.

• You avoid PTA meetings, never visit his school.

• His side is your side in his arguments with teachers.

• Home is a battleground for his parents.

• You expect him to attend religious services but are too busy yourself.

• His allowance is out of line.

• You say, "I'm busy now. Tell me later."

• He is expected to live up to the law while you run through "stop" signs and place bets with a bookie.

• You smile when he scoffs at "squares" and admires those who "get away with it."

• You assume his problems are minor ones.

• White lies are all right for you, but he is expected to tell the whole truth.

• You think the world is against you — and accept it.

• "Let George do it" is your attitude towards charity and community service.

• Election day is a holiday for you; you don't vote.

• Your threatened punishments are not carried out.

• Your punishments are too harsh.

• You are looking for "something for nothing."

• You never admit you could be wrong.

How to Give a Boy a Chance

Juvenile decency calls for more than just prevention of crime. It calls for the making of a good citizen. You can help your youngster and give him a better-than-average chance in life, *if:*

• You avoid the pitfalls on the other list.

• His friends are welcomed or at least known in your home.

- You set aside time to spend with him regularly.
- You also "make" time to listen when he says, "Can I ask you something?"
- He has an outlet for his volcano of energy.
- You recognize the sorry fact that today the street — *any* street in *any* community — is a dangerous place for playing, for meetings of friends, for "hanging around."
- You know where he is, at all times
- There is a curfew in your home, and he has a quiet time to read or study.
- You expect him to assume some responsibilities at home.
- He can count on you for help with his homework — or, at least, an interest in his progress in school.
- You attend religious services with him.
- He is encouraged to perform some community service. As you do.
- Your word to him is your bond — in giving promised rewards and threatened punishments.
- You don't storm when he confesses to minor sins. If you do, you will never hear of the major ones.
- You encourage him in a hobby — something he can do at home or in a group at his Boys' Club.
- He sees you show respect for democratic authority: the local government, his teachers, religious leaders, the police.
- You recognize that nearly every boy has an overwhelming interest in cars — but you believe and stick to it that he should not "go riding with the gang."
- You can exercise a certain amount of censorship over what he reads, what he sees in the movies, his TV viewing.
- You know the places in your community that should be off-limits to the teen-agers — and make sure they are.
- You visit his club on parents' night or whenever he invites you and share his pride in what he is doing.
- You remember how hard it was to be a teen-ager — and you *listen* to what he has to tell you.

Juvenile crime is rising at an alarming rate. Home, church, and school are the major weapons against this appalling situation. Such organizations as Boys' Clubs, Scouts, Little League and PAL are all doing a good job. It is hard, however — and often impossible — to get a boy to turn to an outside organization if he does not receive some encouragement at home.

I am confident that in company with millions of responsible parents you will do your share to see that "juvenile decency" is given every chance to supplant juvenile delinquency.

106. What the Home Should Be (Ps. 133:1; Prov. 5:15; 17:1)

The home has its beginning in the love of two people for each other — a love so real that they forsake all others for each other.

They have different personalities but they learn to adjust to each other's likes and dislikes, virtues and faults. They become a king and queen reigning together over a kingdom.

Into the home children are born and birth is the supreme miracle of the ages. The baby is equally a part of each parent and each has a responsibility toward it.

The home is a *hotel* because it provides a place to sleep. It is a *restaurant* where normally three meals a day are prepared and served. The family shares alike around the table, they feel safe and secure through the night under the protecting roof of their own house.

The home is a *gymnasium* because the child must be provided opportunity to develop his body and keep it strong and healthy.

It is a *school* because that is where the child learns his first and most important lessons.

The home is an *economic institution* because it takes money to keep it going and families learn to share their resources equitably, stretching their dollars to cover their needs, deciding together what they must buy and what they can do without.

The home is a *playground.* In it innocent games are enjoyed, picnics and vacations are planned and in playing together the family is brought closer together.

The home is a *hospital* where numberless bruises are healed, where sick are nursed and where mothers are God-ordained physicians.

The home is a *workshop* where each has duties. The children are given their own job and are made to feel their responsibilities. In the home all are servants and all are served.

It is a *forum* where the family problems are discussed — each one's opinion is heard, where life's problems are freely discussed. It is a perfect democracy where each one is given a place and each one belongs. There is no discrimination in the home.

The home is a *secret society* where family confidences are held and where loyalties are sacred.

Above all, the most important, it is a *temple of worship,* a place where the Bible is the family book, where prayer is heard, where the Heavenly Father is a member of the family, where Christ is exalted.

The home is the most precious possession of mankind. We dare not trifle with its foundation, we give to it our first allegiance. It is no wonder that when man dreams of eternal life, he thinks of that place where our soul lives forever as a home, the house not made with hands, eternal in the heavens.

— Charles L. Allen, *The Houston Chronicle*

107. "Home" . . . The Most Beautiful Word

Scholars of Oxford University in England a few years ago did a research on the most beautiful word in the language. After putting hundreds under scrutiny, they decided that the one word which in its denotation, connotation, and euphony, best exemplified the meaning of beauty was the word — *home.*

108. Home should be more than a filling station.

— W. W. Ayer

109. It takes a hundred men to make an encampment, but one woman can make a home. — *The Speaker's Sourcebook*

110.
> Bless our home,
> Our lives, our friends
> With love that, Lord,
> On Thee depends. Amen.
> — *The Speaker's Sourcebook*

111. Recipe for a Happy Home

To three cups of love and two cups of understanding add four teaspoons of courtesy and two teaspoons each of thoughtfulness and helpfulness. Sift together thoroughly, then stir in an equal amount of work and play. Add three teaspoons of responsibility. Season to taste with study and culture, then fold in a generous amount of worship. Place in pan well greased with security and lined with respect for personality. Sprinkle lightly with a sense of humor. Allow to set in an atmosphere of democratic planning and of mutual sharing. Bake in a moderate oven. When well done, remove and top with a thick coating of Christian teachings. Serve on a platter of friendliness garnished with smiles.

— Pauline and Leonard Miller

112. The home can be the strongest ally of the Sunday School or its greatest enemy, depending on the parents.

— *The Speaker's Sourcebook*

113. A Tribute to a Christian Home

Not long ago a young man in college went home for the weekend. It was unexpected and rather perplexing to the parents, for it was an expensive trip and money was scarce.

But they quietly welcomed him and enjoyed his visit, unquestioning. A day or so after his return to college, they received a letter from him. "I knew you wondered at my coming," he wrote, "but I felt I must. Many things have been disturbing me lately, unsettling my faith, overturning my philosophy, bringing doubt and darkness to my soul. I just had to come home to get within its atmosphere and feel that sureness of everything again. And I found it."

What a tribute to home!   — John E. Price

114. Definitions of the Christian Home
1. Home — A world of strife shut out, a world of love shut in.
2. Home — The place where the small are great and the great are small.
3. Home — The Father's kingdom, the Mother's world, and the child's paradise.
4. Home — Where we grumble the most and are treated the best.
5. Home — The center of our life and affections.

115.   Son, walk the trail you tread
Wherever it may be
So you can come home with lifted head
Back home to her and me.
So live that you can always turn
To where your mother's candles burn,
And not an exile doomed to roam
Some other land — for home is home.
                                    — Douglas Malloch

116. Son to father: "About my allowance, Pop. It's fallen below the national average for teen-agers."

117. The average American works seven minutes for one quart of milk; the Englishman works fourteen minutes, the Russian thirty-three minutes. The average New York shopper can buy with one hour's labor twenty-one times as much sugar, nine times as much butter and four times as much beef as his counterpart in Russia.

118. About 46,400,000 Americans eat in restaurants at least once every week. They spend an average of $2.19 on dinner when they eat out.

119. The average American teen-age boy wolfs $11.30 worth of food a week. Food for his father costs $9.10, for his teen-age sister, $8.80; his mother $7.40; his 8-year-old sister $6.90.

120. "I'm looking for adventure, excitement, beautiful women," cried the young man to his father as he prepared to leave home. "Don't try to stop me."

36

"Who's trying to stop you?" shouted the father. "I'm going with you."

121. Irate father to son: "I sacrificed everything I had so that you could study medicine and this is your thanks. Now that you're a doctor, you tell me I have to quit smoking."

122. Teen talking to friend: "The way I see it, arguing with parents provides you with one of two possibilities. They can be as right as I am, or I can be as wrong as they are."

123. Prov. 1:8
A father tried to give advice . . . As children start to grow . . . The kind of wisdom his own dad . . .Imparted years ago . . . But somehow as he talks to them . . . It does not sound the same . . . And silently he tells himself . . . His efforts are quite lame . . . He wants to teach his youngsters, and . . . To guide them sensibly . . . But feels that he can never match . . . His dad's philosophy . . . And then one day his grown-up son . . . Or daughter with a beau . . . Give thanks to him for some advice . . . Imparted long ago . . . And suddenly it dawns on him . . . And sinks into his head . . . He must have done a little good . . . With something he once said.
— James J. Metcalfe

124. Matt. 7:11; I Peter 4:10
The millionaire's young daughter returned from finishing school and her father gave her a tour of their new mansion. At the swimming pool they stopped to watch several athletic young men diving and stunting.
"Oh, Daddy," she exclaimed, "you've stocked it just for me!"

125. You Learn What You Live With (Hos. 13:6)
If you live with criticism, you learn to condemn . . .
If you live with hostility, you learn to fight . . .
If you live with pity, you learn to feel sorry for yourself . .
If you live with encouragement, you learn to be confident . . .
If you live with fairness, you learn what justice is . . .
If you live with honesty, you learn what truth is . . .
If you live with friendliness, you learn to make friends . . .
If you live with love, you learn to express it . . .
If you live in a Christian home, you learn to cherish Christ.

126. A Lesson Learned (Exod. 20:12; Luke 2:51)
Dear Ann Landers:
I'm a 15-year-old girl with a story to tell.
Last Saturday I was invited to the home of a girl who moved

here recently from Worcester, Mass. Her mother asked me to stay through dinner and I accepted.

I noticed that this girl and her mother treated each other like friends instead of relatives. I felt embarrassed when I heard her talk so politely to her mother because I remembered how I talked to mine.

When this girl's mother got up from the dinner table to fill the milk glasses, she said, "Sit still, Mom. I'll do it." I then remembered how my mother had to tell me three times to fill water glasses before she got any action.

I started on my new plan as soon as I got home. The first thing I did was to straighten my closet and clean my bookcase.

The next day I got up earlier than usual and did all the things I was supposed to do. I spoke very politely to Mom and noticed that in return she was especially nice to me. And it's been that way ever since.

Life is so much more pleasant when people get along together. It's just a matter of respecting one another. I know now that mothers don't enjoy yelling at kids any more than kids enjoy being yelled at. They *want* to have peace in the family, but their kids have to meet them half way. — *Glad I Learned*

— *Houston Chronicle*

127. Great Men Who Overcame Handicaps at Home (Phil. 4:13)

John Adams, second President of the United States, was the son of a grocer of very moderate means. The only start he had was a good education.

Andrew Jackson was born in a log hut in North Carolina, and was reared in the beautiful pine woods for which the state is famous.

James K. Polk spent the earlier years of his life helping to dig a living out of a new farm in North Carolina. He was afterward a clerk in a country store.

Millard Fillmore was the son of a New York farmer, and his home was a humble one. He learned the business of a clothier.

James Buchanan was born in a small town in the Allegheny Mountains. His father cut the logs and built the house in what was then a wilderness.

Abraham Lincoln was the son of a wretchedly poor farmer in Kentucky, and lived in a log cabin until he was twenty-one years old.

Andrew Johnson was apprenticed to a tailor at the age of ten years by his widowed mother. He was never able to attend school, and picked up all the education he ever had.

Ulysses S. Grant lived the life of a village boy, in a plain house on the banks of the Ohio River, until he was seventeen years of age.

James A. Garfield was born in a log cabin. He worked on the farm until he was strong enough to use carpenter's tools, when he learned the trade. He afterwards worked on a canal.

Grover Cleveland's father was a Presbyterian minister with a small salary and a large family. The boys had to earn their living.

William McKinley's early home was plain and comfortable, and his father was able to keep him at school.
— *Rocky Mountain Advocate*

128. When asked how she would describe her relationship with her father, Luci Johnson replied, "Blood."

129. Even the best family tree has its sap.

130. Today's underprivileged child is one who has to share the family car with his parents.

131. When a youth begins to sow wild oats, it's time for father to start the threshing machine.

132. Adolescence is that time of life when children start bringing up their parents. — Barbara Demke

133. Teen-age son to father: "Good news today, Pop!"
Father: "How's that, Son?"
Son, pointing out the door to the family car just wrecked: "You haven't been wasting your money on those automobile-insurance payments!"

134. Definition of Babysitter: A teen-ager who behaves like a grown-up while the grown-ups are out behaving like teen-agers.
— Nancy Bowman, *16 Magazine*

135. Another Language (Ps. 90:12; Isa. 11:2, 3)
In Britain they have published a booklet, *Sixteen,* designed to explain parents to teen-agers. It begins with translations of parent talk. For example, if a parent says, "This is a fine time of night to get home," it means: "I've been worried about you. Why can't you warn me if you're going to be late, so I don't have to sit here imagining all sorts of awful things are happening to you?"

When a parent says, "I don't know what young people are coming to these days," it actually means: "Please tell me a bit more about the way you think and feel, because things are so different nowadays and it's very trying not being able to understand people you love."

136. At a bridal shower, the last gift to be opened was accompanied by a card reading: "May this always be so," and signed, "Much love, Mother and Dad." Inside was a beautifully framed, yellowed piece of paper with childish handwriting on it, which had once graced the bulletin board in the bedroom of the young bride-to-be. There were tears in her eyes as she read us the message:
Today we had a test in history.
I have to go to the dentist, too.
We did not win the paper drive.
This is the worst day I have ever had in my life.

— Clipped

137. A pearl among pebbles is still a pearl.

138. Deut. 24:16
Iphicrates, a shoemaker's son, became a famous Aremian General (325 B.C.). Once he was belittled for his humble ancestry by Harmodius, a descendant of a long line of illustrious people. Iphicrates' reply has become famous. He said, "My family history begins with me, but yours ends with you."

139. If you think we're all born free
You've never paid an obstetrician's fee.

140. Your family: Those who, when you've made a fool of yourself, don't feel that it's a permanent job.

141. An old schoolmaster said to a minister, "I believe the children I teach know the Ten Commandments." The minister asked, "Do they obey them?" The schoolmaster said, "Let's find out." He called on a little boy to repeat the fifth commandment — "Honor thy father and thy mother." The schoolmaster asked, "Tell us, my boy, what this means." The boy blushed. He said, "Yesterday I showed a strange man over the mountain. The sharp stones cut my feet. The man saw they were bleeding. He gave me some money to buy some shoes. I gave it to my mother. She has no shoes either. I thought I could go barefooted better than she could!" In an unselfish way, the boy obeyed the commandment! "Honor thy father and thy mother."

142. A 13-year-old once confided: If I would make changes at my house, I would draw my parents back together. They have been divorced since I was three years old. I would want to have a happy family and go out and do things together as a happy family would.

143. A Teen-age Boy's Candid Opinion:
Of all the people, I admire my father. He is a great old guy. Some people think parents are just for griping at you, but I don't. They are for love and affection.

144. Words of Peace and Power (Prov. 15:23)
I love you
Thank you
I'm sorry
Mom, let me do the dishes tonight.
Dad, relax, I'll run to the store for mom.
For brothers and sisters —
    Forgive me for "jumping down your throat."
    I admire you for . . . .
    To be your brother's keeper takes some doing!

145. Brothers and Sisters Have Value!
No president of the United States has been an only child. All but eight of our presidents were one of four or more kids. All but four have had at least one sister.

146. The key to many of our family problems is the one that fits the family car.

147. "In our family," a little girl told her teacher, "everybody marries relatives. My father married my mother, my uncle married my aunt, and the other day I found out that my grandmother married my grandfather."

148. What to call father —
If he is prominent and wealthy and you stand in awe of him, call him "Father." If he sits in his shirt sleeves and suspenders at ball games, call him "Pop." If he tills the soil and labors in overalls, call him "Pa." If he wheels the baby carriage and carries bundles meekly, call him "Papa," with the accent on the first syllable. If he belongs to a literary circle and writes cultured papers, call him "Papa," with accent on the last syllable. If, however, he makes a pal of you when you're good, and is too wise to let you pull the wool over his loving eyes when you're not, and if, moreover, you're sure no one else you know has quite so fine a father, you may call him "Dad."   —Unknown

149. Like Father, Like Son
Some years ago Emanuel Rosanfield won the Widener Trophy

for catching the largest sailfish weighing 75 lbs. and measuring 7' 10¾". This year the trophy was won by his son who caught a sailfish — you guessed it — 75 lbs. 7' 10¾".

150. The Mathematics of Life
> To work out our life problems,
> We need to *add* love,
> *Subtract* hate,
> *Multiply* good,
> and *Divide* between truth and error!
> —Gayle Erickson, a former student

151. From an Opinion Book (unedited)
Dear Brenda:

You are the best sister in the world. You are my only sister, so I love you very much. Sometimes I may say I hate you, but I always will love you very much.
> Love,
> Rebecca, your sister

152. A mother may play any of the following roles: Teacher, forest ranger, musician, journalist, philosopher, biologist, historian, dramatist, and artist. New York's Chase Manhattan Bank estimates the worth of the average housewife at $3.98 per hour!

153. The only place in some homes where appreciation can be found is in the dictionary.

154. A certain teen-ager discovered that her father had unique ideas about helping her toward maturity, when he declared: This should make you feel even more grown-up — your own phone bill.

155. Many an adult has felt this way:
> If then I could have looked ahead
> As now I can look back
> How many changes I'd have made,
> But I that chance now lack.
> If then I'd known as now I do
> How much good parents mean
> And sister dear and brother, too —
> Oh! what a fool I've been!

156. An Open Letter to a Teen-ager (Phil. 2:4)

Always we hear the plaintive cry of the teen-ager: "What can we do? Where can we go?" The answer is . . . go home! Wash

the windows. . . . Paint the woodwork. . . . Rake the leaves. . . .
Mow the lawn. . . . Wash the car. . . . Learn to cook. . . . Scrub
some floors.

Help the church. . . . Visit the sick. . . . Assist the poor. . . .
Study your lesson. . . . And then when you are through and not
too tired . . . read a book.

Your parents do not owe you entertainment. . . . Your city
does not owe you recreation facilities. . . . The world does not
owe you a living. . . . You owe the world something. . . . You
owe it your time, energy and talents so that no one will be at
war or in poverty, or sick or lonely again.

In plain, simple words: *Grow up;* quit being a crybaby; get
out of your dream world; develop a backbone, and start acting
like a man or a lady.

. . . I'm a parent. I'm tired of nursing, helping, appealing,
begging, excusing, tolerating, denying myself needed comforts for
your every whim and fancy, just because your selfish ego instead
of your common sense dominates your personality, your thinking,
your requests. —Anonymous

157. His status, though regal,
    Has headaches and ills;
He's head of the family,
    But foots all the bills.

158. Nowadays when two newlyweds feather their nest, it's
usually not hard to find four parents who have been plucked!

159. Teen-age girl to friend: "My dad caught me playing ping-
pong in his new white shirt the other day."

Friend: "What happened?"

Teen: "He took the ping-pong paddle away from me and
spanked me with it!"

Friend: "Boy, you were lucky you weren't playing baseball!"

160. Attitudes toward Parental Authority

Dear Abby:

This is for the fourteen-year-old girl who signed herself "Feels
like Cinderella" because she had a twelve o'clock curfew on all
dates.

I am also fourteen and I am not permitted to date at all.
My parents say I can't date until I am sixteen and I don't
think they are strict and old fashioned. They are doing this for
my own good and I love them for it. *Plenty of Time*

161. Dear Abby:

I am twenty and am engaged to be married in June to a boy

43

who is twenty-one. We both live in this city and attend the local college here.

He is allowed to come to my house only three nights a week and he has to be out of the house by 10:30. If we date, I must be home by midnight.

I don't think my parents are unreasonable. I realize they made these restrictions because they know what's best for me and I am grateful. —*White Wedding*

162. Question: I am the product of a very unhappy home. Though I am only eighteen years old, life doesn't seem worth living because my parents are constantly fussing and fighting over trivial matters. They appear to be most immature. Is there anything you can say to people like that? L.G.H.

Answer: It is possible that your parents are both Christians, though it appears somewhat doubtful. If both of them are Christians, then possibly one of them has a very serious nervous disorder that needs treatment. But the most difficult thing in the world is to get people to recognize a need of that kind. They feel insulted if you mention it to them.

At your age it is almost impossible to see things objectively. Be encouraged, because life is worth living but only if you live it for Christ. You do not have to live your life for your parents, and the years that you must spend at home are nearly past. Find a clear objective in life and make. it one that is worth while. Be like the Apostle Paul who said . . . "forgetting those things which are behind, and reaching forth unto those things which are before, I press toward the mark for the prize of the high calling of God in Christ Jesus" (Phil. 3:13, 14). You will be amazed at how many of life's problems are solved once you do this.

Youth today needs a song to sing — a creed to believe! I believe Christ offers all this and more! Trust Him and life will take on a glow that you have never known before. Even in the midst of unhappy circumstances there will be peace and joy. You may even win your parents if they see the change in you.
—Billy Graham

163. In one year the average family of four spends $1,600 for food.

164. The energy contained in the 3,100,000,000 pounds of candy consumed last year in the United States could fly a Boeing-707 40,000,000 miles.

165. The best way to be happy at home is practice your Christianity (at all times)!

166. A teen-ager complained to a friend: "My dad wants me to have all the things he never had when he was a boy — including all A's on my report card."

167. Getting Along with Father
1. "How can I get along better with my father?"
"Mostly by making an effort to do so. Many teen-agers don't really try. Compliment him now and then on the way he does his job or on his ability at sports or a hobby or on being an interesting person. Thank him for something he's done for you. But better, have a chair ready for him to collapse in — if he's not used to compliments!"
2. "Why is it hard to talk to my father?"
"It's probably just as hard for him to talk to you. One reason is that you both use stereotyped expressions that stall talk before it can get going. 'I wish you'd see my point for once,' Dad grumbles. You flip, 'Do we have to go through that bit again?' or just 'Oh yeah?' That chills conversation for good.
"For talk-starters, take something general. It might be an interesting event at school, or get him to tell one of his 'When I was a kid . . . .'"
3. "Why does he always seem so worried?"
"He's in a competitive world and under pressure from many directions. Is he concerned about finances, his business, getting or keeping a job, caring for aging parents, or his own aging? When you learn why he worries, you can understand and sympathize with him. Often you can find ways to ease those worries by coaxing him off to a ball game, by planning a fishing trip to his favorite lake, or by making little gestures, such as tuning in his favorite TV program or bringing home a watermelon as his special treat."
4. "Why is my father so strict?"
"Perhaps because he remembers some wild and thoughtless things he did when young and wants to help you avoid the same hazards."
5. "Why doesn't he treat me as well as other fathers do their sons?"
"He probably does. You see those other fathers and sons only in public, when they're on their best behavior. At home the boys may act less mature, and so the fathers would be much more strict with them."

—From an interview with Dr. Lester A. Kirkendall, Professor of Family Life at Oregon State University

168. Dear Ann Landers:
I would like to reopen the subject of the teen-ager who sat

in front of her house in her boy friend's car for two hours. You said "a car is for transportation. It is not a place to entertain."

It is pathetic when a teen-ager can't invite guests into her living room because of a half-dressed, beer-swizzeling walrus who calls himself a father. One girl wrote about an alcoholic mother who sometimes wore no clothing.

Kids in this spot obviously must find another place to talk. I recommend long walks, the corner malt shop or a coffee house. If the school or church has a recreation room where you can pull up a couple of chairs and chat privately, go there.

169. Famous Men with Humble Backgrounds
Aesop, writer of the famous *Aesop's Fables*, was a slave.
Luther, the great reformer, was son of a miner.
Furguson, the Scottish poet, was son of a humble laborer.
Carey, the well-known missionary, was a shoemaker.
Abraham Lincoln was a rail splitter.

170.
Lives of great men all remind us
We can make our lives sublime,
And departing leave behind us
Footprints in the Sands of Time.
—Longfellow

171. What counts is what you have done, not what kind of family you are from. Abraham Lincoln once remarked: "I care little who my great-grandfather was. I'm much more concerned about who his great-grandson will be."

172. Father: "Well, son, what did you learn in school today?"
Son: "I learned to say 'Yes, sir' and 'No, sir' and 'No, ma'am' and 'Yes, ma'am.'"
Father: "Really?"
Son: "Yeah."

173. A sixteen-year-old girl once wrote: "My pa is such a nice man that I think he must have been a girl when he was a boy."

174. Nowadays you'll find almost everything in the average American home — except the family.

175. Jail Was a Haven for Youth
Pint-sized Clyde Stacks went to jail and found himself a home.
The seventeen-year-old youth — he'll be eighteen in ten more days — got locked up once without trying and a second time because he asked for it.

Clyde, who stands five feet three inches in his bare feet and weighs 111 pounds, told his story at the Houston Police Station.

He had just asked a policeman to lock him up as a vagrant.

He had no home as of early morning, Clyde said, because his mother tossed him out after he was jailed the first time.

"She told me to get the hell out and not come back," Clyde said.

His mother, Mrs. Lucille Stacks, 42, lives in a three-room garage apartment at 115 Pierce Avenue with five other children.

Clyde's story followed a pattern. His father deserted the family five months ago. There was no money, and Clyde had to quit school to help out. That wasn't enough, however, so the family went on relief. Clyde delivered circulars for sixty cents an hour to add to the income after the relief checks were cut from $60 to $25 a week.

Then Friday, his bad luck got worse.

While riding with a nineteen-year-old buddy in an ancient car he was arrested. The car was stopped because its driver was wanted for traffic violations.

Jailed for vagrancy, Clyde looked forward to a hitch on the city P-farm because it was a place to eat and sleep and get a bath. He slept on a cell bunk Friday night.

But Corporation Court Judge J. B. Martin dismissed the vagrancy charge and freed him Saturday morning.

It was when he went home "to wash the jail smell off" that his mother turned him out.

A while later he was seen loafing on the Police Station parking lot and questioned by Patrolman J. E. Freeman who, on Clyde's request, put the boy in jail again for vagrancy.

There he was questioned by Lt. J. O. Brannon. His story touched the officer and Brannon hustled up a change of clothes for Clyde.

Some clean clothes and a bath followed by a haircut from the jail barber, Glenn Claywell, led to another change of luck — this time good.

Jailer L. L. Makwa offered Clyde a temporary home in exchange for doing chores on Makwa's ten-acre place at 11401 Sheridan Road near Lake Houston.

Now all Clyde needs is a birth certificate.

He needs it to join the Navy.

—From *The Houston Post*

---

176. When asked, "Whom do you admire most?" one fourteen-year-old girl said: "The people I admire most are my parents. I admire them because of the way they handle their problems and responsibilities. Whenever they tell me to do something I don't have to question their judgment because they know what's best for me."

177. Father of teen-age son to neighbor: "Junior's at that awkward age — too old for a spanking and too young for analysis."

178. Away from home, a man is judged by what he means — at home, by what he is.

179. The ungrateful son is a wart on his father's face; to leave it is a blemish, to cut it off is painful.   —Chinese Proverb

180. Buying a teen a second-hand car may be one way to teach him how hard it is to drive a bargain!

181.   My teen-age girl emerges
             As a fresh and fragrant bloom,
             No flaws default the whole effect,
             But you should see her room!
                                              — *Sunshine*

182. Modern teen to dad: "But I do too know the value of a dollar. It'll buy about three gallons of gasoline."

183. A fifteen-year-old boy, commenting on his unhappy home life, said: "It has been the same way for fifteen years and if my father didn't holler at me for a week for doing something, or let me go anywhere or do anything I wanted to do, I wouldn't know where to begin and end."

184. From a thirteen-year-old girl:
    Of all the people I've seen and known, I would like to be my mother because I can always come to her with my problems. She is not the type of mother who will get angry because of a bad grade, but instead will help me and see if there are ways to apply what I know and find out what I don't understand.

185. A Chinese Proverb:
    If there is righteousness in the heart, there is beauty in the character. If there is beauty in the character, there will be harmony in the home. If there is harmony in the home, there will be order in the nation. If there is harmony in the nation there will be peace in the world.

186. J. Edgar Hoover, the Chief of our F.B.I., says: "If there is to be peace and happiness in our homes, then we as a nation must turn to God and to the practice of daily family altars."

187. Heading the list of household ills —
Left-over food and left-over bills.

188. An Unusual Definition
My mother was in a dilemma once. She brought home two new hats but my father put his foot down on them. "You want us going bank rupped? You got to take one of them back!" he shouted. So she did, then she bought a dress to go with the hat she kept. My mother is a good dilemma solvur.

—Alison Sainsbury, fifth grader

189. Tomorrow's Parents
Several years ago (1961) two studies cast doubt on the qualifications of today's teen-agers to be competent parents. A group of seventeen thousand high school and college students polled by the Purdue Opinion Panel averaged 40 per cent "wrong" answering questions on childrearing. For example, it is well established that babies need loving care; yet 74 per cent of the teen-age group said that "attention spoils babies." Three-fourths stated that parents should not talk about sex with their children, contrary to the opinion of authorities. In another survey, Dr. H. Frederick Kilander of New York University found that about half of United States college students believe such old wives' tales as the whiskey cure for a fever. About one-third believe that a pregnant mother who listens to good music will have a musical child. A sizeable percentage believes fish is "brain food." Either there isn't enough training for parenthood in school curriculums, or what there is, isn't sinking in, the Purdue researches concluded.

190. That house shall be preserved,
And never shall decay;
Where God and Christ are worshipped,
Day by Day.
— Anonymous

191. Two things I've had in life, and ample — good advice and bad example.

192. Parents, grumbles one teen-ager, are the sum of the squares on both sides of the family.
—"Changing Times," *The Kiplinger Magazine*

193. Life's like this — when you're young your mother tells you what time you have to be home; when you're grown up and married, your babysitter tells you.

194. I like to see a man proud of the place in which he lives. I like to see a man live so that his place will be proud of him.

— Abraham Lincoln

195. Prudence (Prov. 22:3; 15:5)

Never ask of money spent
Where the spender thinks it went.
Nobody was ever meant
To remember or invent
What he did with every cent.
— From the *Complete Poems of Robert Frost*
Published by Holt, Rinehart, and Winston

196. The modern parent has to spare the rod — so Junior can ride in it.

197. Fifteen-year-old Fred: "Dad, the Bible says that if you don't let me have the car, you hate me."

Dad: "Where does it say *that*?"

Son: "Proverbs 13:24. He that spareth the 'rod' hateth his son."

198. A modest pat on the back develops character, if given young enough, often enough, and low enough.

199. We all start the same way.

"Any big men born around here?" asked the tourist in a sarcastic way.

"Nope," replied the native, "best we can do is babies."

200. An elderly Christian once commented, "I have never known a girl who was unfaithful to her mother and shirked home duties that measured up in her responsibilities to her husband in after years. If one of you boys ever come across a girl who says to you as you come to the door, 'I can't go for thirty minutes. The dishes are not washed,' sit right down and wait for that girl. Cherish her. Woo her. Win her before some other fellow gets her. Stick to her like a burr sticks to a mule's tail!"

201. A boy is the only thing God can use to make a man.

I I I.

EXPANDING MENTAL
HORIZONS

202. I Kings 11:28; Gal. 6:9.

Robert Louis Stevenson to stepson:

"I am not a man of any unusual talent; I started out with very moderate abilities. My success has been due to my really remarkable industry; to developing what I had in me to the extreme limit. When a man begins to sharpen one faculty and keeps on sharpening it with tireless perseverance, he can achieve wonders. Everybody knows it; it's a commonplace. And yet how rare it is to find anybody doing it — I mean to the uttermost as I did. What genius I had was for work."

203. Glad and Sorry (I Sam. 9:27; Ps. 1:2; I Thess. 4:11)

One night, in ancient times, three horsemen were riding across a desert. As they crossed the dry bed of a river, out of the darkness a voice called, "Halt!"

They obeyed. The voice then told them to dismount, pick up a handful of pebbles, put the pebbles in their pockets and remount.

The voice then said, "You have done as I commanded. Tomorrow at sun-up you will be both glad and sorry." Mystified, the horsemen rode on.

When the sun rose, they reached into their pockets and found that a miracle had happened. The pebbles had been transformed into diamonds, rubies, and other precious stones. They remembered the warning. They were both glad and sorry — glad they had taken some, and sorry they had not taken more . . . .

And this is a story of education.

— Dr. L. H. Adolfson
Director Extension Division, University of Wisconsin

204. Study to show thyself approved unto God, a workman that needeth not to be ashamed, rightly dividing the word of truth.

— II Timothy 2:15

205. Unless some students begin studying harder, their high school diplomas will have to be gift-wrapped.

206. "The Teacher's Pet"

> I love to do my homework,
> It makes me feel so good;
> I love to do exactly
> As my teachers say I should.
>
> I love my schoolwork very much,
> I never miss a day;
> I even love the men in white
> Who are taking me away!

207. Facts about the Non-High School Graduate (Jer. 32:33)
- Gets only the poorest jobs which offer little or no promotion.
- Works long hours at jobs that are hard and uninteresting.
- Must face heavy competition even for the worst jobs, as at this moment, there are one million jobless young people between sixteen and twenty-five.
- Has a choice of only four out of one hundred jobs that require no education.
- Suffers with a low standard of living.
- Puts his future family on the wrong side of the tracks, with a shabby hut in which to live, and an old jalopy to drive.

208. Monetary Value of Education

Paul C. Glick of the United States Census Bureau points out that a high school graduate earns $49,000 more in his lifetime than does the fellow who quit after the eighth grade.

He also reveals that each year of college adds an additional $25,000 to lifetime income. This means that a college graduate earns $103,000 more than even the high school graduate. Incidentally, a recent report by a research organization stated that every day in college is worth $92.59!

209. Three million seven hundred and twenty-eight thousand eighteen-year-olds will graduate next June (1965). Presently, there are 24.2 million teens in America.

210. You might think that college degrees, since they're increasingly common, wouldn't make as much difference in income any more. Not so. In 1956-57, the average family head with a degree earned $8,500 a year, $3,400 more than the typical high school graduate; now he averages $11,070 — $5,330 more.

> — Lawrence Galton, *Houston Post*
> November 12, 1964

211. Disappointed student: "Not only did I get bad grades, but I was on the wrong side of the room during the tooth paste test."

212. When the son of a TV star came home with his report card, his father asked, "Well, son, were you promoted?"

"Better than that," said the boy, "I was held over for another twenty-six weeks."

213. A teen-ager appended this notation at the end of his test paper: "The views expressed here are not necessarily those of the textbook."

214. A high schooler handed his not-so-good report card to his father. Looking the card over, the father said, "One thing is in your favor, son. It's evident you haven't been cheating."

215. A teen-ager claims that a kiss definitely has a place in the English class, because

A kiss is a noun because it is both common and proper.

A kiss is a pronoun because she stands for it.

A kiss is a verb because it is either active or passive.

216. Deut. 12:30; I Cor. 10:6

Double-Slaying "Inspired" by French Novel, Lawman Says

Los Angeles (UPI), October 9, 1965 — An 18 year old philosophy major was being held without bail today for the double slaying of two workmen, which assertedly had been inspired by a French existentialist novel.

Wayne Welch, a former high school honor student, was taken into custody Friday for the fatal shooting of Alejandro Lopez Montez, 57, and John M. Kimball, 51.

Lt. Earl A. Deemer said Welch told him he was inspired to commit the crime after reading Albert Camus' novel, *The Stranger,* which describes the murder of an Arab on a beach and the murderer's subsequent emotions.

Lt. Deemer said Welch told him he selected the two victims at random, just to try out the slaying depicted in the novel.

The pages described in Camus' powerful prose the emotions that rage in the novel's protagonist as he shoots the stranger on the beach.

Detectives said Welch apparently sought to experience some similar emotion when he fired one bullet into Montez and two into Kimball, with no other apparent motive.

Camus had won the Nobel Prize for Literature in 1957 for his "Clear-sighted earnestness [which] illuminates the problems of the human conscience in our times."

— *Houston Chronicle,* October 9, 1965

". . . Everything began to reel before my eyes. A fiery gust came from the sea, while the sky cracked in two, from end to

53

end, and a great sheet of flame poured down through the rift. Every nerve in my body was a steel spring, and my grip closed on the revolver. The trigger gave, and the smooth underbelly of the butt jogged my palm. And so, with that crisp shipcrack sound, it all began. . . ."   — From *The Stranger*, by Albert Camus

217. Matt. 15:19; II Tim. 3:1, 2

Earlier this year, a New Jersey High School assigned its advanced senior English students the reading of the 202-page paperback, *Franny and Zooey*, by J. D. Salinger. The copyright page of the book shows that it passed through twelve printings between August, 1961, and October, 1962.

Liberally sprinkled with revolting expressions, this book appears to be an effort to cheapen and downgrade God for the purpose of destroying reverence. The main characters of the book curse continually, but worse than that, the author himself engages in piratical cursing in a transition paragraph between two sections of dialogue.

The attitude of many of our educators seems to be that young people must be exposed to this type of book if they are to face the literary realities of our time. This is tantamount to claiming that one must walk through the sewers of a city in order to be exposed to the realities of urban life.

— *Christian Economics*

218. Alibi-ography for Students (Luke 14:18)

When you are asked or assigned this —	Say this —
When you are given an objective test —	"It doesn't let you express yourself."
When you are given an essay test —	"It's so vague. You don't know what's expected."
When you are given many minor tests —	"Why not have a few big tests? This keeps you on edge all the time."
When you are given no tests —	"It's not fair. How can he possibly judge what you know."
When every part of the subject is taken up in class —	"Oh, he just follows the book."
When you are asked to study a part of the subject by yourself —	"Why, we never even discussed it!"

Robert Tyson, Dept. of Psychology, Hunter College

219. Num. 13; 14:1-25; Heb. 10:35

A high school physics teacher once told a certain teen that a football could only be thrown a certain distance. "Fifty yards," he said, "is as far as anyone can throw the thing. I've made certain calculations, taken unto account the shape of the ball, and that is the top distance that it can be thrown."

The youth got a football and took the teacher outside to a field. He threw the pigskin as far as he could. Then they measured the distance — seventy-three yards on the fly! The boy's name? Frank Ryan, who eventually became quarterback for the world champion Cleveland Browns professional football team.

220. To see how times have changed all you have to do is make a comparison. It used to be that a teen-age boy let his best girl wear his ring. Now he lets her borrow his hair curlers.

221.

Year	Education	Began Work at	Work Life	Lifetime Earnings
1920	3 years of high school	16	34 years	$120,000
1940	High school graduate	18	38 years	$265,000
1960	1-3 years of college	20	43 years	$470,000

222.
One should not love money,
Of that I have no doubt.
    But I'm just as sure
    Being poor's no cure —
I'd rather be with than without.
              — L. O. C.

223.
Procrastination is my sin,
It causes me endless sorrow.
But I've made up my mind to quit,
And I will begin — tomorrow.
              — Anonymous

224. Indispensable
Sometimes, when you're feeling important,
    Sometimes, when your ego's in bloom,
Sometimes, when you take it for granted
    You're the best qualified in the room;

Sometimes, when you feel that your going
    Would leave an unfillable hole,
Just follow this simple instruction
    And see how it humbles your soul:

Take a bucket and fill it with water,
Put your hand in it, up to your wrist;
Pull it out — and the hole that's remaining
Is the measure of how you'll be missed.
— Anonymous

225.
Can one think and not wonder?
I wonder.
Can one wonder and not think?
I wonder.
But the wonder is to think.
I think.

226. Some Tips on Good Discipline (especially for classroom teachers)

1. Have only a few rules. Be sure they are necessary and in the general interest, not just for your comfort, and be sure everyone knows what they are. Enforce them without emotion or commotion.

2. Be consistent and impartial. Don't have pets who get away with things others cannot. It shouldn't make any difference who does it — what is done and under what circumstances should make the difference.

3. Don't argue with a pupil. Enforce the rules.

4. Don't nag. If you are going to cut a dog's tail off, do it all at once — don't cut it off an inch at a time.

5. Certainty of punishment is more of a deterrent than severity.

6. It is better to be strict with new groups at the beginning. It is easier to loosen up as the school year progresses than it is to tighten up.

7. Stop the little things. It is easier to put out a match than it is a forest fire.

8. Take it for granted that the class is well-intentioned. If you expect trouble, you'll probably get it.

9. Don't make threats you can't carry out; such as, "If you do that again, you'll be sent to the office and I won't take you back."

10. Don't be afraid to acknowledge an error. You are not infallible, and the class knows it.

11. Don't discipline an entire class for the misconduct of a few individuals.

12. There is a difference between being friendly and being familiar. Observe it.

13. Study your class before making a final seating arrangement.

14. Remember that true discipline is self-discipline. This should be your goal, and you should make it clear to the pupils.

15. Sarcasm and ridicule have no place in the high-school classroom.

16. If you get satisfaction from punishing a child, you are probably being unfair.

17. In punishing a pupil, never speak disrespectfully of his parents or his home training.

18. Make use of the pivotal figures in the room, the ones who enjoy high regard in the eyes of the student body. Win them and you win the class, but don't bribe them with favors.

19. Discipline is not necessarily synonymous with punishment. Some teachers achieve good discipline by a system of rewards and privileges. Pupils who are disorderly are deprived of privileges.

20. Watch the "mechanics" of classroom management. Do the pupils have too little or too much light? Are they facing the light? Is it too warm, too cold or too stuffy in the room?

21. Be tolerant of passing fancies. There isn't just one way to wear your hair or to dress. The teacher who makes a fuss about teen-age fads and styles in hair-do or dress is swimming against a strong current. They'll improve. Give them a chance to grow up.

22. Remember that since the ultimate goal of all discipline is self-restraint, you above all should exemplify it. Too often, teachers who advocate severe discipline are themselves intemperate in their actions and rash in their judgments. They interpret any misconduct as directed at them personally, regarding it as a deliberate, defiant, intolerable personal insult. It is not unusual to see such a teacher usher an offender to the principal's office demanding that prompt reprisal be administered, in the teacher's presence and according to the teacher's demands.

— John M. Gran, *How to Understand and Teach Teen-Agers*,
T. S. Denison and Company, pp. 95-97 (used by permission)

227. Son to Father: "Checking scholarships, investigating grants, looking into awards, exploring student loans — it's the modern method of working your way through college, Pop."

228. Wisdom and Ignorance (Prov. 29:11; I Cor. 3:18; 8:2)
>Wisdom goes looking for a light,
>And speaks not till that light is glowing,
>Ignorance claims by day and night
>It has all knowledge worth knowing.
>
>All things that perish or endure
>Give us alike this implication:
>Ignorance only is cocksure,
>While wisdom knows its limitation.
>—Clarence Edwin Flynn

229. Wernher von Braun: "Unless he improves, he will fail."
(Job 23:8; Eccles. 7:8)

If you have trouble with mathematics, don't worry. Rocket expert Wernher von Braun did too when he was a boy.

His father, Baron Magnus von Braun, at eighty-four, an imposing man with a short white beard, recalled at Oberaudorf, Germany, that his son failed the ninth grade because he wasn't interested in the arithmetic and kindred subjects he later found essential to his career.

"The failure came as no surprise because his teachers' quarterly reports said he had little interest in the subject," the baron said.

With a chuckle he recalled the wording of one report: "Unless he improves, he will fail."

It was later at the Hermann Lietz High School at Speikeroog, on the North Sea, that the trend changed.

"When I opened a letter from the school I got a big surprise," the father said proudly. "It said Wernher was ahead of his class in mathematics and that his progress was remarkable.

"Later I was told that he had substituted for a sick teacher and taught the final school year in mathematics."

230. In baseball you can fail to get a hit two out of every three times at bat and make any major league team in the world.

231. Slogan posted on wall of college students' lounge: I know all the answers — its the *questions* I don't understand.

232. Joe (with coin in hand) to roommate: "If it's heads, we go to bed. If it's tails, we stay up. If it stands on edge, we study."

233. An Impractical Theory (Gal. 6:7)

When the teacher in a high school class in economics found that his pupils were in favor of the theory of taking from those who had more than enough, and giving to those in need, he announced that beginning immediately, he would put the system in operation in class. He would subtract from the grades of the top students, and add it to the grades of the poorest students, so all would get an average grade.

The first month the system worked pretty well. The grades of the best students were high enough to offset the deficiency of the lower ones, and the class average was above the passing mark. Then the situation changed.

The top students saw no reason to put forth extra effort required to get good grades, with which they would not be credited.

The medium students put forth less effort for they were assured passing grades.

The dullards did not work at all, since they would pass with the aid of the grades from the others.

So, while at first the system provided passing grades for all, within a very short time the entire class was failing. They then realized that this socialistic-communistic theory was impractical.

234. Gen. 11:7; Ps. 71:1; I Peter 2:6

One youngster, obviously in a hurry on a school assignment, wrote to the *National Geographic*: "Would you get all the information you could possibly get and send it to me in less time as possible?"

Another youngster wrote: "I am no help to my teachers because I have no research information. I would appreciate it very much if you could send me anything about anything."

— *Sunshine*

235. Teacher: "Is there any difference between results and consequences?"

Student: "Well, my experience has been that results are what you expect; consequences are what you get."

236. Girl Dropouts

Each year approximately half of the one million Americans who quit high school before graduating are girls. In some areas the proportion is as high as two-thirds. And these hundreds of thousands of young girls make up the most forlorn and forgotten segment of our society.

True, boy dropouts may commit more dramatic crimes. But girl dropouts — though "nicer" and "smarter" as a group — are probably more self-destructive. When girls quit school, they doom themselves. They become jobless, lost, bewildered, defeated, hopeless, rejected, drifting outsiders of society — "fugitives from failure," Dr. Daniel Schreiber, director of the National Education Association's pioneering School Dropout Project, calls them. Some plunge into senseless sex or run off to a hasty marriage. Others enter a harsh world that has no place for them. Nearly nine out of ten report afterwards they regret quitting.

Not surprisingly, a vast number of dropouts wind up on relief rolls. In Cook County, Illinois, 85 per cent of those receiving aid never finished high school. Studies indicate the figure elsewhere runs as high as 90 per cent. Dropouts also make up a large percentage of the 250,000 women who bear illegitimate children every year — 90,000 of whom are teen-agers and 5,000 of whom are under fifteen. This is partly because many schools follow a rigid policy of automatically expelling girls when they become pregnant and do little to encourage them to return to school after the baby is born. This is especially shortsighted, because the girl may now need education more than ever in order to earn a living for herself and the baby.

Why do most girls quit school?

By far the largest number claim they drop out to marry or because they wish to marry. According to one estimate, about 200,000 girls aged fifteen to seventeen each year forsake the road to learning for the bridal path.

Sadly, these marriages turn out much less successfully than others. One study shows that dropouts tend to marry dropouts, thus perpetuating the breed. And when they do not marry dropouts the results may be worse. One expert cites the case of Alice who, when Fred finished high school, quit to marry him. For a time they were happy. But Fred, an alert and ambitious young man who realized that he needed more education, enrolled for night courses. Often his college friends gathered at his home. Alice, good wife that she tried to be, quietly filled the coffee cups and listened to them talk about things she did not understand. She felt left out. As the time went on, a gap developed between Alice and her husband. They seemed to have less and less to say to each other. The final result was heartbreak for Alice and divorce.

A second big reason why girls quit school is rebellion against their parents. An intensive Chicago study of intellectually capable dropouts, directed by Dr. Solomon Lichter, found that, "The majority of girls were rebelling and acting out hostilities against problems at home not only in school but in other social areas of their lives. They became aggressive and defiant in the face of any authority. Truancy, one of the ways they expressed their rebellion, was a frequent problem and often came as a complete surprise to their parents."

A third important reason why girls (as well as boys) drop out is what Dr. Schreiber terms "adverse school experience." This includes failing grades, getting behind and feeling discouraged, dissatisfaction with the school program — especially the lack of desired vocational training — moving from one school to another, rejection by classmates or the school staff and, of course, reading retardation.

Some teachers give up too easily on the potential dropout. Dr. K. B. Hoyt of Iowa State University, president of the American Personnel and Guidance Association, deplores this attitude as one of "teach the best and shoot the rest."

What is being done to help girl dropouts?

A dramatic effort now is being made by Uncle Sam through

the Job Corps, in the Office of Economic Opportunity, an arm of the Johnson Administration's war on poverty. It is now operating five residential training centers for about fifteen hundred girls in Cleveland; Charleston, West Virginia; Los Angeles; Omaha; and St. Petersburg. Officials hope to have fourteen centers accommodating five thousand girls at this year's end and to reach one hundred thousand next year. The aim is to make these girls useful, responsible citizens.

At the centers girl dropouts receive guidance, academic and vocational training including basic instruction in reading, speech and mathematics. They are taught business and clerical skills and child and home care.

Dr. Bennetta B. Washington, director of the training centers, a former Washington, D.C., high school principal who was nationally acclaimed for helping hundreds of young people stay in school, told *Parade*: "These girl dropouts don't know who they are, what they can be or what they want to be. They are afraid, but they don't know of what. They are angry, but they don't know at whom. They're rejected and they don't know why. All they want is to be somebody."

We must try harder to break this vicious cycle of human waste where the girl dropout becomes the frustrated woman — and the next generation pays the price.

For, as Mrs. Lyndon Johnson has said, "When you teach a man, you teach an individual. But when you teach a woman, you teach a family."

— Jack Harrison Pollack
Condensed from *Parade*, September 26, 1965

237. A college student with some knowledge of Bible history wrote the following lines in one of his textbooks:

If there should be more flood,
For refuge hither fly:
Though all the world should be submerged
This book will still be dry.

238. *Grades.* Is there any correlation between school grades and success? Are the best positions in life occupied by men and women who made the best grades in school? A research study of 1,072 leaders in finance, education, and government listed in *Who's Who in America*, shows a majority of these leaders averaged C-plus to B in college.

— *Parade*, May 23, 1965

239. Teacher: "What is practical nursing?"
Pupil: "Falling in love with a rich patient."

240. Notes on proverbs that contradict each other:

On the one hand, "Don't put all your eggs in one basket," but on the other, "In union there is strength."

"Opposites attract," but, "Birds of a feather flock together."

"Absence makes the heart grow fonder," but, "Out of sight, out of mind."

"Haste makes waste," but, "He who hesitates is lost."

"Two heads are better than one," but, "Too many cooks spoil the broth."

"A straight line is the shortest distance between two points," but, "The longest way 'round is the shortest way home."

241. Many a child who watches television for hours will go down in history — not to mention arithmetic, English, and geography.

242. One of the Secrets of Success (Acts 24:16)

Once Michelangelo, painting frescoes in the Sistine Chapel, was lying on his back on a high scaffold, carefully outlining a figure in a corner of the ceiling. A friend asked him why he took such pains with a figure that would be so great a distance away from the viewer. "After all," said the friend, "who will know whether it is perfect or not?" "I will," said the artist.

243. Attention (I Cor. 7:35)

There is one thing we can do and the happiest people are those who do it to the limit of their ability.

We can be completely present. We can be all there. We can control the tendency of our minds to wander from the situation we are in toward yesterday, toward tomorrow, and toward something we have forgotten, toward some other place we are going next. It is hard to do this, but it is harder to understand afterward wherein it was we fell so short. It was where and when we ceased to give our entire attention to the person, the opportunity, before us. — Mark Van Doren

244. Jer. 48:41

Phil Summers, Green River High School quarterback (Green River, Wyoming), waited all season to try a certain play. It worked one Friday night last season.

Summers called out to the referee, "Haven't we got a five-yard penalty on this?" then took the ball from his center and started stepping off yardage against Evanston High.

Summers didn't stop until he'd run 71 yards through the bewildered Evanston football team for a touchdown, giving Green River the margin it needed to win, 20-13, in an upset.

Coach Jerry McMillan said Summers pestered him all season

to try the play. "I didn't think it would work," McMillan admitted.

245. Boy: "If you were offered a choice between ham and eggs and a million dollars, which would you choose?"
Friend: "A million dollars, of course."
Boy: "I'd rather have the ham and eggs."
Friend: "Why?"
Boy: "Simple. Nothing is better than a million dollars and ham and eggs is better than nothing."

246. He who does not know history must repeat man's mistakes.
— Santayana

247. "History" may be rightly divided "His story."

248.
I put my faith and trust in you
I thought I could rely.
But now I'm disillusioned —
I wish that I might die.
I made you my ideal, you see
And so I copied you.
I should have copied someone else
For now I'm flunking, too!
— *Sunshine*

249. Wise as Serpents (Eccles. 9:18)
Missionary Bruce E. Porterfield tells in his new book, *Command for Christ*, how false teeth may save a man's life or cause his death. A missionary friend of his was about to be killed. Suddenly he had an inspiration. He hit himself hard on the head several times, twisted his ears, and pulled down on his chair. Then he removed his teeth. Never having seen a man take out all his teeth, the natives' minds were diverted. They began imitating his actions and forgot all about killing him.

Porterfield has had some hair-raising experiences himself. In an interview he said that once an Indian of a stone-age tribe in Bolivia examined his hair, ears, nose and skin. Then he thrust his hand into his mouth and began exploring the inside much to the missionary's dismay because of his dentures. He was afraid that the Indian might succeed in removing them and would be so fascinated he would keep them. His only alternative was to repulse him, which might arouse the savage's rage and result in his death.

Porterfield said, "These split-second decisions constantly face us one way or another. I decided to bite him hard. He drew back in hostility, his friendship gone, but I doubled over with laughter to indicate this was my idea of a rough sort of horseplay and he accepted it that way."

250. I Kings 3:12; Prov. 4:7

According to a poll in San Diego, the average American high school girl has stopped lionizing the captain of the football team, prefers to date the boy with brains. According to Dr. Orrin Klapp, who supervised the survey: "The young intellectual is in."

251. English Is Easy?
We'll begin with box, the plural is boxes,
But the plural of ox is oxen, not oxes;
One fowl is a goose, but two are called geese,
Yet the plural of moose is never meese;
You may find a lone mouse or a whole nest of mice,
But the plural of house is houses, not hice.
If the plural of man is always men,
Why shouldn't the plural of pan be called pen?
If I speak of a foot and you show me two feet,
And I give you a boot, would a pair be called beet?
If the singular's this and the plural these,
Should the plural of kiss ever be keese?
We speak of a brother and also of brethren,
But though we say mother, we never say methren.
Then the masculine pronouns are he, his and him,
But imagine the feminine, she, shis and shim!
Any questions?   — *Sottish Rite News*

252. The quickest way for a child to get attention in school these days is for him to bend his IBM card.

253. A lecture is something that can make you feel numb at one end and dumb at the other.

254. Checking up on Dad's Brag
Providence, R.I. (AP) — Bryant College officials recently received the following letter from a son of one of their most illustrious alumni:
"Dear Sir:

"Could you please send me a copy of the marks of —. I am his son and he is bragging about his marks. He graduated from Bryant College in 1950. I am a student in the 8th grade. I would appreciate if you would respond immediately as my report card is coming soon.

"Yours truly,
— Jr."

255. Teacher to small pupil presenting petition for signature: "Sorry, Tommy — I can't sign a test-ban agreement."

256. According to the experts, during the 1960's, 7½ million young people will quit school and 2½ million will not even finish grade school.

257. Teen-ager: Somebody who thinks the three R's are a Rock-n-Roll group.

258. Parent: "My daughter has failed driving tests five times this semester."

Neighbor: "Is she quitting?"

Parent: "No, but her instructor has applied for a transfer to another school."

259. The following sayings have been handed down to us through the ages: "The Greatest Word is God." "The Longest Word is Eternity." And "The Strongest Word is Right." But couldn't we add this one last saying to the list: "The Happiest Word is Service."

> — From a speech on Service by Galen Hope, Finalist in an
> American Legion Award's Contest, Deady Jr. High, 1965

260. The human mind is an enormous storeroom that can be filled for one's good with knowledge, goodness, fairness, and love. A scholarly boy or girl is not always someone born brilliant; he is usually a person who obtains his good grades by hard work, diligence, and accuracy. A true scholar never thinks he knows everything for he realizes the fact that all knowledge can never be obtained.

Knowledge is wealth. "There is no wealth like unto knowledge, thieves cannot steal it." "A man is poor not because he has nothing but because he does nothing with what he has." You are rich by your knowledge of things and although they may not have large monetary value, almost everything you learn improves you and helps to build you into a better person. Knowledge is power for as the Bible says, "Ye shall know the truth and the truth shall make you free."

> — From a speech on Scholarship by
> Cindy Maerz, American Legion Award Winner

261. Report card evaluations by teachers and classmates do not always give a true indication of what to expect from a youth when he leaves school. For example:

Thomas A. Edison was sent home from school one day with a

note from his teacher stating that he was such a dunce that he could never be expected to learn anything!

Charles Darwin could never learn a foreign language.

Napoleon was number forty-two in his class at school.

Sir Isaac Newton was next to the lowest in his class.

George Eliot learned to read with great difficulty and gave in youth no evidence of brilliance.

James Russell Lowell was suspended from Harvard for "Complete indolence."

James Watt, inventor of the steam engine, was frequently the victim of his classmates' jokes at school.

Winston Churchill rated last academically in his class at Harrow; by his name were the lowest marks in the entire school!

262. When asked, "What is your son taking up at college?" one father replied, "Space."

263. In explaining her tardiness to English class, a high school junior stated demurely, "The boy who was following me walked very slowly."

264. A columnist named Mike Royko who writes for the *Chicago Daily News* received a letter from a teen-ager who felt that not enough recognition was being given teen-agers.

"Dear Good Teen-Ager: I am sick of you. You are getting to be a pain in the neck.

"I can't remember the last time a Good Teen-ager came up to me and shook my hand and said, 'Gee, Good Adult, thanks for not being a Bad Adult.'

"You say nobody understands you and points out how valiantly you have resisted being a robber, a sniffer of glue, a drop-out, and a menace to society. Besides, you don't hit your teacher, and you work after school and are a joy to your parents.

"I do not go around taking pep pills or shooting people either. My reward is that I don't get put in jail and is also your reward. You don't punch your teacher and I don't punch my boss. So you get an education and I get to keep my job. You don't hot rod your car and neither do I. We both may live longer and that is a pretty nice reward, isn't it?

"You work after school, I work after work. We both get money which is always handy to have around. And don't forget for many years I have been contributing part of my money to building those schools that you are so generously not dropping out of.

"Your reward for staying in school is an education which will help you hold down a better job or be a doctor or a lawyer.

"Education can help you live a fuller life and be a Good Adult. So stop writing and asking for praise for doing what you are supposed to do. That's what you're here for."

"Yours truly,
Mike Royko"

265. College Requirements (I Tim. 4:8b)

The Educational Records Bureau of New York City made a survey to find the criteria on which students are admitted to college. Their information was secured from 560 questionnaires. The report was that the College Board Scholastic Aptitude Test is not the number one consideration for admittance to college. The considerations were as follows:

1. High school grade record.
2. Recommendation of the school principal or counselor.
3. College Board Scholastic Aptitude Test
4. Applicant's class standing.

Nine out of ten colleges want information about the student's character, his emotional stability, attitudes, and leadership qualities. Many colleges pay more attention to the personal qualities of the applicant than they did ten years ago. Eighty per cent of the colleges include results of personal interviews in admission decisions.

From this it is recognizable that a student's personal character and standard of values is an important criterion. Good scholarship records and recommendations from the administrative staff are based on the total record of the student.

— *Vision*

266. Everyone Has a Weakness (James 5:16; Job 2:3)

Albert Einstein once admitted that figuring out his United States income tax was beyond him — he had to go to a tax consultant. "This is too difficult for a mathematician," said Einstein. "It takes a philosopher."

267. The Honor Roll (I Cor. 14:19)

A certain high school in Arizona, announcing its month's honor roll, explained thus: "A student whose average exhibited performance in all credited subjects in relation to the performance of all other students falls at a level which places him (or her) on the normal curve of probability at a point falling on the plus side of the mean and between the second and third standard deviations will have made the honor roll first class."

268. Many people have the right aim in life, but they never pull the trigger.

269. Minds are like parachutes; they only function when they are open.

270. He Knew What Is Most Important

Many years ago a young man from western Pennsylvania decided that he wanted to go to Princeton University because he had been deeply impressed by what he had heard of its president. He took the examination and failed, but before returning to his home decided that he would try to see President McCosh.

So he called at the president's home, and Mr. McCosh came to the door. The young man told him that he had planned to enter Princeton and had not been able to meet the requirements, but before going home wished to thank him for what he had learned there.

President McCosh said, "Mon, what hae ye learned from us?" The young man replied, "How little I know!" "Mon, we will take ye," Mr. McCosh answered. "Ye are two years ahead of the rest of them." —Thomas Dreier

271. What's the Object? (I Peter 3:15)
Teacher: "John, give me a sentence with a direct object."
John: "Teacher, everybody thinks you're beautiful."
Teacher: "Thank you, John, but what is the object?"
John: "A good report card."

272. Silence is the only successful substitute for brains.

273. "The greater the obstacle the more the glory in overcoming it." — Moliere

274. It is through each of us, as persons, that all greatness springs; great art, great music, great accomplishments of a nation are born in the mind of the person. It is the Person through whom God has chosen to manifest Himself. —Conrad N. Hilton

275. In America today, three-quarters of a million youngsters every year drop out before they graduate from high school.

The facts indicate that half or more of dropouts have normal IQ or better. And nearly one out of five has 120 IQ or more.

Even worse, Educational Testing Service says that fifty thousand "are among the nation's potentially most able students."

276. Job 28:13; Phil. 3:7
Two brothers, one a famous baseball pitcher, the other a minister, met after a long separation. Some time was spent in exchange of reminiscences of bygone days.

Finally the minister said, "How is it, Bill — I spent four years in college and three years in the seminary, and you've never done anything but play ball. Now you're getting a salary of thirty thousand, and I'm getting three. I can't understand."

Bill thought a minute, then said, "I'll tell you how it is, Jim. It's all in the delivery!" —*Sunshine*

277. The college drop-out rate in this country is approximately 60 per cent.

278. It is better to try to do something and fail than try to do nothing and succeed.

279. Schools were never intended to be tranquilizers; they should be agitators.

280. More Thoughts on Preparation
Luck is what happens when preparation meets opportunity.
If you fail to prepare, prepare to fail.
"I will prepare and someday my chance will come."
 —Abraham Lincoln
Dig a well before you get thirsty. —Chinese Proverb

281. Ps. 19:12; John 12:16; I Peter 3:16
"I don't think you have the slightest idea what punctuation means," the English teacher said to a student, who replied, "Indeed I have! I'm·here every morning at five minutes to eight!"

282. Henry Townley Heald, President of Ford Foundation:
"Education's real challenge is to produce men and women who know how to think; and knowing how, do it; and having done it, voice their opinions."

283. Originality: What a good thing Adam had — when he said a thing he knew nobody had said it before.
 —Mark Twain

284. To become educated doesn't mean you have to become refrigerated! Informed Christians develop enthusiasm, instead of losing it.

285. Lincoln: My great concern is not whether you have failed, but whether you are content with your failure."

286. Edison failed ten thousand times before inventing the incandescent bulb. He saw the bright side, however, for he discovered ten thousand things that wouldn't work.

287. II Sam. 19:35; Gal. 6:10

Recently an attempt to block teen-agers from running for public office died in the Massachusetts Legislature shortly after a smiling sixteen-year-old filed his candidacy for state representative.

A vote in the House to admit a late-filed bill to ban all teen-age office seekers failed to achieve the necessary four-fifths majority.

Leonard E. Tagg of North Weymouth filed nomination papers containing 892 signatures, 180 more than he needed, earlier Friday.

Tagg is running as an independent through a legal loophole that could have been plugged by the house bill.

House Republican leaders led the fight to block the bill, saying existing laws ban minors from running for public office.

Tagg and two companions sat on the side of the house chamber during the debate.

Tagg, while doing research for a high school thesis, discovered that the state law provides that a Democratic or Republican candidate must be twenty-one years old, but it says nothing about independents.   —*Houston Chronicle,* July 4, 1964

288. Opportunity (Prov. 3:21, 23)

Every year young folks spend in high school, can be worth $17,500 to each of them, according to the United States Chamber of Commerce. A full four years can be worth $70,000. That is the extra amount they will probably earn on an average over their working lives by going to school.

289. To ensure the education of teen-agers, parents need to pull a few wires: television, telephone, and ignition.

290. Mathematics is the alphabet with which God has written the universe.   —Galileo

291. The boy who best learns all he can will best succeed when he's a man.

292. Teen Ingenuity (Dan. 1:4)

In Wyandotte, Michigan, a seventeen-year-old high school girl tested the United States Post Office's gentleness with packages — and the Post Office flunked.

For a science-fair project, for which she won a blue ribbon, Carol Skrycki mailed eight accelerometers, devices which measure sharp movements, to a California collaborator. The instruments showed that jolts equal to a three-foot drop had been sustained by boxes marked "air mail special delivery fragile" and "air mail special delivery" as well as one package deliberately left unmarked. In packages marked "air mail," "fragile," or "second class," the accelerometers showed the effects of a five-foot drop.

Carol could not report on the jolts undergone by the parcels she had marked "first class" and "third class." Both were smashed flat by the time they reached California, and the devices were broken. —Clipped

293. It Takes More than Desire (Deut. 1:41; Acts 7:30-32, 34)

Some young people are mistakenly led to believe that God's calling "for their lives is that which seems presently convenient and that which requires as little effort as possible to fulfill."

A teen-ager, whom God has called into the ministry, recently told me, "I don't have time to go to school and study. The Lord may come tomorrow, and I've got to be about my Father's business now."

You know what that reminds me of? Something like this: Here's a fellow with extremely high fever, and a severe pain in his stomach. The doctor says he must have his appendix removed or he will die.

All of a sudden a young man runs up to the bedside holding a sharp knife. He explains to the patient, "I'm not a real doctor — I haven't qualified myself by going to medical school, but I do want to help suffering humanity. Do you mind if I remove your appendix?"

Crazy, you say? It's not any more foolish than the person who thinks he can help the human soul without much study, training and prayer! —L.O.C.

294. It is by education I learn to do by choice, what other men do by the constraint of fear. —Aristotle

295. All who have meditated on the art of governing mankind have been convinced that the fate of empires depends on the education of youth. —Aristotle

296. Jails and prisons are the complement of schools; so many less that you have of the latter, so many more must you have of the former. —H. Mann

297. 'Tis education forms the common mind; just as the twig is bent the tree is inclined. —Pope

298. The chief purpose of education is to train the mind and the will to do the work that needs to be done, when it needs to be done, whether one likes it or not. —Huxley

299. What sculpture is to a block of marble, education is to the human soul. The philosopher, the saint, the hero, the wise, and the good or great, very often lie hid and concealed in a plebeian, which a proper education might have disinterred and brought to light. —Addison

300. Education does not mean teaching people to know what they do not know; it means teaching them to behave as they do not behave. —Ruskin

301. The first thing education teaches you is to walk alone.
—Trader Horn

302. There are obviously two educations. One should teach us how to live and the other how to make a living.
—James Truslow Adams

303. To know the laws of God in nature and revelation, and then to fashion the affections and will into harmony with those laws — this is education. —S. F. Scovel

304. Knowledge does not comprise all which is contained in the large terms of education. The feelings are to be disciplined; the passions are to be restrained; true and worthy motives are to be inspired; a profound religious feeling is to be instilled, and pure morality inculcated under all circumstances. All this is comprised in education. —Daniel Webster

305. Education is not learning; it is the exercise and development of the mind; and the two great methods by which this end may be accomplished are in the halls of learning, or in the conflicts of life. —*Princeton Review*

306. Eccles. 11:6; Isa. 28:10; Acts 21:37; Rom. 15:2
She talks for hours of Edgar Poe,
And tells me stuff I oughta know.
She tries to make my grammar good,
To use them pronouns as I should.
Sometimes we have a spelling meet
And I'm the first guy to his seat.
And when she calls me to recite,
Them things I learnt jes' don't seem right,
And when she thinks I'm awful dumb
And after school she makes me come
Into her room where I recite
Them words until it's almost night.
And then next day she gives a test.
And I'm the guy what flunks the best.

But supposin' things should change a wee.
And for a spell I might teach she.
I'd open class down by the brook,
And teach her how to bait a hook.
"Ya take the worm like this," I'd say,
"Now, put it on the hook this way."
(I think she'd probably squirm with fright
Like me, when she'd make me recite.)
And when we'd both get on my boat,
And soon as all was calm and quiet
We'd catch a frog and learn his diet.
She'd sure pick up a fact or three
If she'd but take a course from me.
I may be dumb 'bout punctuation,
But there's lotsa kinds of education!
—Prudence Platt, Student,
North (Kansas City, Mo.) High
School, in *NEA Journal*

307. "A genius is usually a crackpot until he hits the jackpot."

308. Consider the feelings of the father whose son became such a problem at school that he was sent home with a note from the principal, to wit: "Please send a written excuse for your son's presence!"

309. Speaking at a school banquet, Stewart Harral of the University of Oklahoma confessed, "Professors are not any smarter than other people. We just have our ignorance better organized."

310. I can't help but wonder just how many commencement speakers dressed in identical black suits stand up before graduates in identical robes and square hats and exhort them not to follow the crowd, but dare to be individuals.
—Bob Stanley, *Journal-Republican*

311. Why is it that there is never enough time to do it right, but there is always enough time to do it over!   —Mark Twain

312. Prof: "If there are any dumbbells in the room, please stand up." A long pause. Then a lone freshman stood up in the rear.
"What — do you consider yourself a dumbbell?" asked the Prof.
"Well, not exactly," replied the freshman, "but I hate to see you standing all alone."

BUILDING MORE MATURE
FRIENDSHIPS

313. Ps. 19:14; Mark 14:70; Col. 4:6

For those who are having trouble understanding teens, a partial glossary of teen talk follows:

Words	Translations
rock out, un-cool, beat, black, down-the-tube, square, launchy, grabby, pain, bomb	Bad
wipe out	to fail or make a major mistake
kangaroos, kickens	shoes
a ring or a bell	telephone
cut buddy	best friend
shadow	constant companion
a hustle	a job
green bark, lettuce	money
scab, shank, out, or dog	unattractive and unpopular girls
shooting the tube	perfect
riding the same wave	togetherness
golden gasser	old-time hit song
"What's your mob adjustment?"	"How're you feeling?"
"I was shot down."	"I failed the exam."
a real cool set of threads	attractive sport coat
"Let's put it in orbit."	"Let's go"
Grimmie	Someone who pretends to be something he isn't
pad	house or room
hang to	to do something outstanding
grounded	loss of all privileges and rights, like telephone, TV and dates.

314. The Three S's of Popularity (Gen. 11:4)

Every normal person asks the question, "How can I be popular?" because one of the deepest desires of the human heart is the love and appreciation of other people.

On the other hand universal popularity is impossible to obtain. We have different denominations because we disagree on matters of theology and church policy. On such questions as what amusements a Christian might enjoy, how to spend Sunday, race relations, politics; in fact on any question we do have different opinions. Some people like classical music. Others enjoy the "hillbilly" type of music. Some "gentlemen prefer blonds," others prefer brunettes, and some like red-heads the best.

So no matter what position you take, some will approve and some will disapprove. Unfortunately, most of us have not yet learned to love the person who holds different opinions from our own.

We respect people because of what the person is. It is better to win respect than popularity. Someone has said, "The world buys you for what you think you are worth."

However, self-respect does not mean conceit. The One who said, "I am the bread of life"; "I am the light of the world," took a towel, got on His knees and washed the feet of other men. "What God wants is men great enough to be small enough to be used." As Phillips Brooks said, "The true way to be humble is to stand at your real height against some higher nature."

To win the respect of others we must be sincere. Clovis Chappel points out that the word sincere comes from two Latin words: *sine* — "without" and *cera* — "wax." When a defective piece of marble was taken from the quarry in the long ago, there were certain dishonest dealers who could skillfully cover over the defect with wax and make it appear perfect. But when the piece was put into a building the rains and the winds would eventually show up that defect. So honest dealers would stamp their marble *sine-cera*. There were no covered-over defects.

To win respect we must forget ourselves. Why is it we admire our mothers? Isn't it because she forgot herself in our interest? In America we have developed the "go-getter" spirit. More and more we are saying, "It's not how you play but whether or not you win the game." Success has come to be one of our gods.

But study the lives of those the world has called great. You will find that, though they are different in many ways, all the truly great people had one thing in common. They all lived saying, "I came not into this world to be ministered unto but to minister."

No person ever becomes great until he finds something greater than himself for which he is willing to give himself. The wisest One who ever lived said, "He that loseth his life for my sake shall find it."

Respect is better than popularity, and self-respect, sincerity and service is the way to get it.

—Charles L. Allen. Adapted
from the *Houston Chronicle*

315. A man, Sir, should keep his friendships in constant repair.
—Samuel Johnson

316.
      The man that hails you Tom or Jack,
      And proves by thumps upon your back
          How he esteems your merit,
      Is such a friend, that one had need
      Be very much his friend indeed
          To pardon or to bear it.
—William Cowper

317.
      Who friendship with a knave hath made
      Is judged a partner in the trade.
—John Gay

318. It is more shameful to mistrust one's friends than to be deceived by them. — La Rochefoucauld

319. True friendship is a plant of slow growth, and must undergo and withstand the shocks of adversity before it is entitled to the appellation. —George Washington

320. A friend is someone who knows all about you and likes you just the same.

321. Acts 2:22; 4:12
Now the person celebrated in the Gospels is the greatest personality in history. He was the greatest nerve specialist who ever lived. "Come unto me . . . and you shall find rest unto your souls." His way is incomparably the best way; it is the way to peace of mind, to courage, independence, fearlessness, to joy. If we find faith lacking, try His way.
—William Lyon Phelps, *Marriage,* pp. 45, 46.

322. Prov. 22:1
In his first public speech, Abraham Lincoln said to the voters of Sagamon County, "I have no other ambition so great as that of being esteemed by my fellow men."

323. John 5:44; I Cor. 9:24; 4:1
Dr. Charles L. Allen tells in his book, *In Quest of God's Power,* of a high school girl who was elected class president. "How did it happen?" her father asked. She replied, "It didn't happen, I happened it."

324.
      Not what we give but what we share,
      The gift without the giver is bare.

325. During a flood a rooster and skunk were seen together floating on a bale of hay. The lesson? You never know who you'll have to buddy-up with when trouble comes.

326. People are not any more difficult to get along with in one place than another, and "Getting along" depends about 98 per cent on one's own behavior.   —Wilfred A. Peterson

327. I Sam. 9:2; Luke 2:40; I Thess. 4:10

Dr. Thomas E. Cone, associate clinical professor of pediatrics at Harvard Medical School, believes that many severe social problems of today's teen-agers may merely be a reflection of their earlier biological maturity. The maturation of teen biological functions is being experienced earlier than ever before, dropping two to three months every decade for the past fifty to seventy years. An example given by Dr. Cone was in regard to the menstrual period, which is more commonly beginning at the age of eleven. From this it follows that earlier dating and other social activities "may not be due entirely to social pressure by parents, but simply an outgrowth of this earlier maturity."

According to Dr. Cone, a marked increase in height of American children has been noted since the first large-scale measurements of youngsters was taken in 1877. Today's ten-year-old is as tall as the twelve-year-old was in 1877.

What is causing this increase in size? Better quality and distribution of food, higher living standards and control of diseases.

> —From a speech given November 14, 1965, at the closing session of the Pediatric Postgraduate Symposium in Texas Children's Hospital, Houston, Texas

328. Fourteen Billion dollars — annual teen income.

Five hundred sixty-five thousand American teen girls own their own car.

Nine million teens own their own phonograph and buy records regularly.

One million teens have completed school and have a steady income.   —*Conquest*

329. Youth is the time of the possible.

> —Juliette Low, founder of the Girl Scouts

330. A boy may not realize when he's falling in love, but he's about the only one who doesn't.   —*News,* Bowie, Texas

331.   Mary had a little slam
            For everyone and so —
         The leaves of her engagement book
            Were just as white as snow.

332. Better be unknown than ill-known.

333. A teen-ager is known by the company he keeps — out of.

334. Medicine Man. A young African becoming a Christian turned over three fetishes to a missionary. One was a bottle of medicine which he said had protected him on journeys; one was a nut filled with medicine which he claimed had protected him against beatings by colonial administrators; and the third was a root which he said had "got him his girl friends." When the missionary returned to the States, he brought the fetishes with him, and when he spoke before various congregations frequently passed them around for the parishioners to see. "Somehow, somewhere," he reports, "the root disappeared."   — Selected

335. Then there was the teen whose spirit was so low that he told his buddy, "The only way I can feel superior is by seeing that my inferiority complex is bigger than any one else's."

336. Wonder how things would change if starting a romance took as much skill as ending it?

337. A survey by the Girl Guides reports that by age thirteen, one out of ten American girls are wearing lipstick and using perfume.

338. Some are not popular because they don't talk enough; others, because they talk too much! As to which weakness is greater, the following poem contains instructions:
            You'll rank as quite a hit among
               Your friends if you've a ready
               tongue.
            But you'll be rated still more dear
               If you possess a ready ear.

339. Friendship is to be purchased only by friendship.
                                        —Thomas Wilson

340. What is a Friend? I will tell you. It is a person with whom you dare to be yourself.   —Frank Crane

341. They are rich who have true friends.   —Thomas Fuller

342. He will never have true friends who is afraid of making enemies.   —William Hazlitt

343. I do desire we may be better strangers.
        —William Shakespeare

344.   Men are polished, through act and speech,
          Each by each,
      As pebbles are smoothed on the rolling beach.
        —J. T. Trowbridge

345. He who begins to be your friend because it pays will also cease because it pays.   —Seneca

346. Nothing is more annoying than a tardy friend.   —Plautus

347. Ps. 4:6; Isa. 65:22; Phil. 4:8
    Two buckets met at a well one day. One bucket had a big smile on its face. The other had a big frown.
    "Why are you frowning?" asked the happy bucket.
    "Oh, no matter how full I am when I leave the well, I always return empty," complained the sad bucket.
    "And why are you always smiling," asked the unhappy bucket.
    "No matter how empty I am when I come to the well, I always leave full!"

348. The world is a looking glass, and gives back to every man the reflection of his own face. Frown at it, and it will in turn look sourly upon you; smile at it and it is a jolly, kind companion.

349. The Golden Rule Acted Out (Prov. 11:25; Rom. 12:10)
                Do all the good you can,
                By all the means you can,
                In all the ways you can,
                In all the places you can,
                At all the times you can,
                To all the people you can,
                As long as ever you can.

350. The reason the average girl would rather have beauty than brains is that the average guy can see better than he can think.

351. One of the easiest ways to become popular is to remember the nice things folks say about a person, and repeat them to him.

352. Bad Examples Can Serve (I Tim. 4:12)

If you want to avoid unattractive manners, watch the other fellow.

A sensitive character should impress you with the fact that being easily wounded is usually an unbecoming form of conceit.

An egocentric person talking incessantly of "me, myself and I" is a forceful reminder never to allow yourself to become self-centered.

A person who consistently displays poor taste in dress should point the fact that, if you are not a natural in correct styling, you should adopt the habit of seeking a consultant.

Poor posture in others is a frightening suggestion that you too may develop slovenliness.

That one who delights in criticism of others provides an illustrated lecture on the tiresomeness of such an inelegant sport.

The individual who cannot be trusted with a secret should teach you the value of belonging to a minority group who can be trusted with a confidence.   — Anne Bell Miller

353. The weaker sex is the stronger sex because of the weakness of the stronger sex for the weaker sex.

354. Matt. 13:14; I John 3:16

In matters controversial
My perception's always fine.
I always see both points of view;
The one that's wrong and mine.
                    —*Houston Post,* June 1, 1964

355. Prov. 4:7; II Cor. 1:6

He: "Will you marry me?"
She: "No, but I'll always admire your good taste."

356. Don't throw away the old bucket until you know whether the new one holds water.

357. Job 32:18; I Peter 5:12

A teen-aged farmer had planted a crop of flax, and had a tablecloth made from the linen he produced. Sometime later he remarked to his sophisticated sixteen-year-old cousin from the city:

"I grew this tablecloth myself."

"Did you really?" the cousin remarked with a little sarcasm. "How do you ever manage to grow such things?"

"Promise you won't tell?" he asked.

She promised.

"Well," he whispered solemnly, "I planted a napkin."

358. The Mathematics of Popularity

1. *Add* a kind word about someone to each conversation. Someone has said, "Keep your words sweet; you might have to eat them."

2. *Subtract* from other people's cares and worries by doing what you can to help them. "Bear ye one another's burdens."

3. *Multiply* by zero your tendency to criticize and to be overly proud. Your answer tells you how often this should happen in the future.

4. *Divide* your happiness with others by sharing it with them. You keep only what you give away; what you try to keep for yourself you lose.
—L.O.C.

359. Most of us would rather be ruined by praise than saved by criticism.

360. Lord Chesterfield in His Letters to His Son

Make other people like themselves a little better, my son, and I promise you they will like you very well.

361. A girl becomes a woman when she stops looking for the ideal man and starts looking for a husband.

362. Handling Disagreements (Prov. 15:1)

A little explained, a little endured,
A little forgiven, the quarrel is cured.

363. Steel that loses its temper is worthless — so are men.

364. Easy to Please (Judg. 16:4-21; I Cor. 9:22)

A fifteen-year-old approached his girl friend with one hand cupped over the other. "Jan," he said, "if you can guess what I have in my hand, I'll take you out tonight."

"An elephant?" Jan asked.

"Nope," he replied. "But that's close enough. Pick you up at 7:30."

365. Some things a fellow will never have unless he makes them himself — friends.

366. It was said of one girl that she has broken up so many "steadies" that she's listed in the Yellow pages under "Demolition Experts."

367. He who has nothing but virtues is not much better than he who has nothing but faults.

368. Good Friend of Mine (I Sam. 18:1; Prov. 17:17)
I'd like to be the sort of friend that you have been to me,
I'd like to be the help that you are always glad to be,
I'd like to mean as much to you each minute of the day
As you have meant, Good Friend of Mine, to me along the way;
I'm wishing at this special time that I could but repay,
A portion of the gladness that you've strewn along my way;
If I could have but just one wish, this only would it be,
I'd like to be the sort of friend that you have been to me!
—Anonymous

369. The more we approach an enemy, the more the tigers of
the heart become lambs. —Chinese proverb

370. An impossible person is one who thinks almost as much of
himself as you do of yourself.

371. Marriage Hangs by a Thread (Matt. 19:6)
One of the world's most curious divorce laws is enforced by
the Balante of French Portugal and Portuguese Guinea. Their
marriages last as long as the bride's wedding gown. As soon as
it becomes threadbare the marriage is dead. If the bride is happy
she wears the gown so little that it will last a long time. If she is
unhappy she sees to it that it is soon worn out.

372. Do not be ashamed of mistakes and thus make them
crimes. —Chinese proverb

373. Glass, China and Reputation are easily crack'd, and never
well mended. —Ben Franklin

374. FHA Survey on Marriage (II Cor. 6:14, 17)
Future Homemakers of America meeting here this week have
found that love ranks fourth among ingredients necessary for a
successful marriage.

375. "Similar-religious backgrounds" and "completed education"
were listed as the top essentials in a survey made by the FHA
among 360 young married couples.
Sharon, a recent Felfry (Ky.) high school graduate, said
the third most often named factor in the personal interviews was
sufficient maturity. — *Houston Chronicle,* July 14, 1964

376. A teen-ager sent his girl friend her first orchid with this
note: "With all my love and most of my allowance."

377. You may talk too much on the best of subjects.
—Ben Franklin

378. Changing Times (Ps. 122:6; Matt. 6:21)

Noticing how eagerly my teen-age daughter fights down every obstacle in her path to answer the telephone on the first ring, I told her that in my day girls used to wait for the third or fourth ring so they wouldn't appear too anxious. "Goodness, Mom!" she retorted, "that was before the age of status symbols. Do you want everyone to think I live in an underphoned home?"

379. He that falls in love with himself will have no rivals.

—Ben Franklin

380. Don't bother to boast of your work to others; the work itself has a much better voice.

381. Our Lips and Ears (Ps. 19:14; Luke 14:11; Col. 4:6)

> If you your lips would keep from slips
>   Five things observe with care:
> Of whom you speak, to whom you speak,
>   And how and when and where.
>
> If you your ears would save from jeers,
>   These things keep kindly hid:
> Myself and I, and mine and my,
>   And how I do and did.   —Unknown

382. Some teen-agers never make out-going phone calls — for fear they'll miss an incoming one.

383. Jer. 2:32; I Tim. 2:8, 9

Two golfers, strangers to each other, happened to meet on the golf links. "See that girl over there?" said one. "Imagine her parents allowing her to appear in clothes like that. Just copying men's clothes."

"That, sir, is my daughter," said the second golfer.

"Oh, pardon me. I'm sorry. I didn't know you were her father."

"I'm not. I'm her mother!"   *—The Kablegram*

384. Discretion (Gen. 41:39; Hos. 14:9; Titus 2:4, 5)

Farm Girl: "I'm afraid to walk through the woods with you, Abner. You might kiss me."

Farm boy: "Shucks, with me carrying a bucket, a cane, and a chicken and leading a lamb, how could I?"

Farm girl: "Well, you might stick the cane in the ground, tie the lamb to it, and put the chicken under the bucket."

— Texas Outlook

385. Half of the troubles of this life can be traced to saying yes too quick and not saying no soon enough.

—Josh Billings

386. Emerson said of Lincoln: "His heart was as great as the world, but there was no room in it to hold the memory of a wrong."

387. Prov. 3:7; 30:13; Isa. 65:5

Then there was the self-builder who when courtesies of the ministry were extended to him, intended to say, "The Lord has called me to heal the sick, cast out devils, and raise the dead." But instead he said, ". . . heal the dead, cast out sick, and raise the devil."

388. Lord, help us to take advantage of an opportunity and not the people who offer them.

389. Most of us know how to say nothing; few of us when.

390. A fashion expert says, "You dress the way you think and you act the way you dress."

391. Three-tenths of good looks are due to nature; seven-tenths to dress.

392. A fifty-year survey of marriage trends by the Population Reference Bureau, Washington, D.C., reveals that American brides and grooms are now "younger and closer in age at first marriage than are those in any other major urban-industrial country in the world." Parents who don't want their daughters to marry at eighteen, the age at which most of them are marrying, should try to get them into college. On the average, a college education delays a girl's marriage four years, to twenty-two, which is the most common marriage age for women college graduates. For high school graduates, eighteen is the wedding age, and for women who did not attend high school, fourteen to sixteen. (John 2:1, 2)

393. If a girl really likes a man, money doesn't make any difference — unless, of course, he doesn't have any.

394. If you have a chip on your shoulder, that's a sign you have wood higher up!!

395. Les Giblin, writer: "The Speech Research Unit of Kenyon College proved through tests that when a person is shouted at, he simply cannot help but shout back. . . . You can use this scientific knowledge to keep another person from becoming angry; control the other person's tone of voice by your own voice. Psychology has proved that if you keep your voice soft, you will not become angry. Psychology has accepted as scientific the old Biblical injunction, 'A soft answer turneth away wrath.'"

396. The girl who searches too long for a smart cookie is apt to wind up with a crumb.

397. Ps. 119:45; I Cor. 8:9
Coed: "Daddy, the girl who sits next to me in class has a dress just like mine."
Dad: "So you want a new dress."
Coed: "Well, it would be cheaper than changing colleges."

398. "It is better for the sheep to have the wolf as enemy than as friend."

399. Ps. 33:1

> Each time we meet, you always say
>   Some word of praise that makes me gay.
> You see some hidden, struggling trait,
>   Encourage it and make it great.
> Tight-fisted little buds of good
>   Bloom large because you said they would.
> A glad, mad music in me sings;
>   My soul sprouts tiny flaming wings
> My day takes on a brand-new zest.
>   Your gift of praising brings my best,
> Revives my spirit, flings it high;
>   For God loves praise, and so do I.
> — Author Unknown

400. Fifteen is the most likely age at which the lonely child, desperate to be loved and accepted, attempts suicide.

— *Parade*

401. Girls and Athletic Success (II Cor. 8:11; I Tim. 4:7)
A football coach at a certain junior high school says girls and football don't mix. In fact, he frowns on his players' associating with girls and warns them that they'll get booted off the team if they talk with them in the school corridors. "I definitely don't want them with girls and they know it," he said. He says he doesn't think kids at the junior high age are mature enough to mix studies, girls and football. "The grades come first, then football, and that's it," he said. "I've told them that if they want to play football, don't talk to girls. I've had a few problems but I

haven't disciplined anyone yet for being with girls." So far this season, the coach's girl-snubbing team has won one game and lost five.

402. Some people pay so much attention to their reputation that they lose their character.

403. Value of a Smile (I Kings 21:7)
A smile costs nothing, but gives much. It enriches those who receive, without making poorer those who give. It takes but a moment, but the memory of it sometimes lasts forever. None is so rich or mighty that he can get along without it and none is so poor but that he can be made rich by it.

— Anonymous

404. Whether you win or lose friends may depend upon whether your opinion is candid or can*died*.

405. The only thing that children can wear out faster than shoes is parents.   — McKenzie, *Squibs and Quips*

406. The following rules for social success appeared in a high school newspaper in California:
1. Have a car
2. Be a pleasant conversationalist
3. Have a car
4. Be congenial
5. Have a car
6. Be a good listener
7. Have a car
Numbers 2, 4, and 6 can be omitted if the car is a red convertible.

407. A college survey sampled how sensitive teen-agers are to what others think of them. Part of the results showed the following attitudes:
• Twenty-six per cent felt that "more than anything I want to be accepted as a member the group that's most popular at school."
• Twenty-nine per cent confessed "I want to be something just to make people like me."
• Thirty-eight per cent thought "nothing is worse than being considered 'odd ball' by my own age groups."
• Fifty per cent disclosed "I am greatly upset if my group doesn't approve of me."
• Twenty-six per cent stated "I quite often disagree with group opinion."

408. A close examination of young people polled revealed that the 26 per cent who "quite often disagreed with group opinion" were the real leaders. They had learned to think for themselves. They refused to become slaves to public opinion, conforming their convictions and activities to "what they think." James Russell Lowell has said, "They are slaves who dare not be in the right with two or three."

409. Jed: "Your sister is spoiled, isn't she?"
Ted: "No, that's the perfume she uses."

410. A high school boy took home from the library a book whose cover read *How to Hug*, only to discover that it was Volume 7 of an encyclopedia!

411. "Do you have the book, *Man, Master of Women?*" a young man asked the lady librarian.
"Fiction counter to your left," the librarian replied.

412. "Girls," the manager of the restaurant said, "I want you all to look your best today. Greet every customer with a smile, put on a little extra makeup, and see that your hair is attractive."
"What's up?" one gal asked. "Are some big shots coming in today?"
"No," the manager answered. "The beef's tough."

413. The teen-ager was weighing herself while her date looked on. She made a wry face.
He asked, "What's the matter? Are you overweight?"
"No, not that," she replied, "but according to this chart, I should be six inches taller."

414. Prejudice is a great time-saver. It enables us to form opinions without bothering with facts.

415. There is a difference between friends you can count up and those you can count on.

416. Happiness is not getting what you want, but wanting what you get.

417. Prov. 22:1; Job 32:21; James 2:23
A survey of teens conducted by *Scholastic* magazine revealed that:
• Thirty-three per cent objected to being called "egghead."
• Less than four per cent would balk at being called "millionaires" or "wall streeters."

- Thirty-eight per cent would be happy to be known as democrats or liberals.

- Forty-four per cent liked idea of being called republican, conservative, or capitalist.

418. The word "chicken" has created more than its share of trouble. The youngster who accepts a dare, who goes along to be part of the crowd, is a constant figure in our courts. A seventeen-year-old high school girl went out with a young man who took her to a party of his friends, all older than she. Marijuana cigarettes were passed around. She refused one at first but finally yielded to taunts of "chicken" and later went with her new boyfriend to two similar parties. The last one was raided by the police. The girl was placed on probation and will always have a record.

Too many youngsters seem to look on the standards of society as a crisscross of fences to hem them in. They do not realize that our laws are, in fact, signposts to a good, full life.

— Excerpted from "Hijinks That Can Haunt Your Life"
by Judge Jerome M. Lasky, *The Christian Herald*

419. Hos. 10:13; Heb. 11:25

What are the two most widespread communicable diseases in America today? And what age is experiencing the greatest number of new infections? According to Dr. William J. Brown, Chief VD Branch, United States Public Health Service, the answers are as follows: (1) Syphilis and gonorrhea ranging from fifteen to twenty. (2) Teen-agers, their age accounts for 56 per cent of the victims, a staggering thirteen hundred a day — namely one every minute!

Dr. Luther Terry, United States Surgeon General, warns that "these facts are merely a token of what lies ahead."

Ignorance regarding the facts about VD are indicated by the following popular, but mistaken, ideas:

"If you picked up VD you would know it."
"Nice kids from nice homes don't contact VD."
"It's always the girl who passes this disease to a man."
"VD is connected with filth or lack of bodily hygiene."
"A shot of penicillin and your worries are over."

Single young people who abstain from sexual relations have no trouble with VD. The syphilis germ will die within five seconds if exposed to sun and air. So it is highly unlikely to pick up this infection from a toilet seat, eating utensils or drinking glasses, or from shaking hands with an infected person. The disease is passed on to another if the germ came in contact with a sore, a crack in the skin, or a cut. Infection is caused almost without exception by sexual contact with an infected person.

> — An adaptation from
> "Why the Rise in Teen-Age Venereal Disease,"
> by L. Edward Maxwell, *Today's Health*, September, 1965

420. "She said 'No' too late." (I Sam. 26:21; Eccles. 2:13; I Cor. 3:17)

"Most girls talk about sex a lot among themselves, and if you're inexperienced, you start wanting to find out what all the shouting's about. At least that's how it was in my high school. The other girls talked like they knew everything, and soon I decided I had to experiment to keep up with them.

"The next date I had was with a boy from our church youth group, so I figured he'd be safe to experiment on. I didn't really care about him as someone special, so I figured if things got embarrassing, I could cut him out of my life without regret. He was expendable.

"We went to the movies, and then we parked to watch the view. I encouraged him. We necked for over an hour, and it was all I could do to keep from laughing out loud. I was completely unaffected, simply following the directions I'd heard the other girls discuss, and there he was, breathing hard and trembling. Nothing happened though, because he was a good guy.

"I was vaguely aware that I'd been cruel to him. I know I wasn't proud of myself, but I kept testing out the other guys I dated in a similar way.

"I was lucky until I reached nineteen, and then things blew up one night. I'd been dating this boy for a year, and I figured I could handle him without any trouble. Perhaps it was the fact that I'd tried to break off a week earlier, or maybe it was just a backlog of pressure. Anyhow we necked for an hour and a half that night, and then suddenly he was pushing me to go all the way.

"I told him 'No.' Then I told him again 'No!' And still he kept at me. I tried to get out of the car, and he flipped and started beating me. I screamed and then he really rained blows on my stomach, face and arms.

"I guess he must have hit my windpipe then, because I blacked out. Have you ever done that? Well, it's the worst; I thought I was dying, no breath.

"The boy resuscitated me then and after I stopped crying he took me home.

"Now, let me emphasize again that he was no thug. He was a church boy who planned to be a minister. The whole experience was horrible for him.

"Apparently he felt so terrible about it that he just blocked it out of his mind and refused to admit that it had ever happened. He couldn't understand why I wouldn't date him any more. For myself, it was over two years before I could stand to let a guy get close to me again!

"Girls need to realize that boys have a much lower boiling point than we do. When it's still casual fun and games to us, it's already the main event for the boys.

"Some girls say, 'If the boy really loves you, he'll respect you enough to stop before — well, before . . ., but actually I believe many guys do push girls they love to go all the way. It's not because they want to exploit the girls, it's just because genuine caring results in love-making that continues far beyond the fellows' point of self-control.

"If I had to make my point in a single paragraph, I'd say this. 'Girls, have respect for the power of your womanhood. Sure, it gives you a kick to see that you can affect a guy and make him want you; but have consideration for his feelings, too. If you're not willing to go all the way, don't give him the feeling that it's a free and easy road, then suddenly throw up a road block that may send him into an emotional tailspin. It's unfair and unsafe.'"

— A letter from a university coed to
    Ely and Walt Dulaney, *Houston Post,* January 8, 1965
    Reprinted by permission of Bell-McClure Syndicate

421. Eavesdropping on Some Handy Hints for Men (Ps. 90:12; Luke 12:33)

Things a young man rarely thinks about until it's too late, and he has married the girl:

Whether she can cook, or is interested in learning how to do more than warm up a frozen dinner.

Whether she is energetic, or just naturally lazy.

Whether she is fond of children or whether they drive her crazy.

Whether she likes things neat and tidy or doesn't mind ever-lasting clutter.

Whether she can entertain herself by reading or working at a hobby, or needs constant entertainment because she hates to be alone.

Whether she had enough curiosity and interest to want to go on learning all of her life, or is satisfied with what she learned in school.

Whether she has a happy disposition or is miserable a lot of the time.

Whether she can meet trouble courageously, or goes to pieces when things go wrong.

Whether she really wants to get married, or just wants to get away from home.

Whether she will always have to have her way to be happy, or will be willing to give in to others' wishes some of the time. It's usually after marriage that a man begins to notice such things, and then it's a little late. — Ruth Millet

422. You can always tell a boy's nationality when you introduce him to a pretty girl.

A French boy will kiss her hand
An English boy will shake her hand
An American boy will ask for a date
A Russian boy will wire Moscow for instructions

423. Two beatniks were talking about what they would like to be if they had a choice.

"If I had my way," said one, "I'd like to play third base for the New York Yankees!"

"Why third base?" asked the other.

"Well, picture sixty thousand fans some Sunday, and me on third. Bases are loaded, and Colavito doubles to left. One run scores, two runs score! Then the throw comes to me. But I hold the ball. The third run scores, and even Colavito crosses the plate! Just imagine those sixty thousand fans screaming, 'You idiot! You crazy fool!' Think of it, man what — *recognition!*"

— Selected

424. Teacher: "What would you call a marriage in which the husband is entitled to only one wife?"

High School girl: "Monotony."

425. English major to pal: "Define Wolf."

Pal: "You tell me."

English major: "A guy who treats all women as sequels."

426. Many a little squirt thinks he's a fountain of wisdom.

427. Braggart

When he opens his mouth
To air his conceits,
In goes his foot
And out come his feats!
— Anonymous

428. Tongue-tied (Ps. 34:4; I Cor. 2:3; II Tim. 1:7)
> If I am asked to stand and speak unto a group,
> The blood deserts my ruddy cheek and turns to soup.
> Confusion I just can't disguise. I long to flee!
> Oh, that I were two other guys instead of me!
> I can't think of a single word — I want to sneeze!
> The only sound from me that's heard is knocking knees.
> But when I'm seated my heart sings! I'm free from dread.
> And then I think of brilliant things I could have said!
> — *Sunshine*

429. If, when you stand before a group to speak your knees knock, don't worry. It's when your knees begin missing each other that the worrying should start!

430. Waiter: "May I help you with that soup, sir?"
Diner: "What do you mean? I don't need any help."
Waiter: "Sorry, sir. From the sound I thought you might wish to be dragged ashore."

431. Among mortals, who is faultless?

432. The surest way to gain respect is to earn it by good conduct.
> — McKenzie, *1600 Squibs and Quips*

433. It is better for a young man to blush than to turn pale.
> — Cicero

434. A psychiatrist says that talking will cure a lot of our troubles. No one believes it. Talking was what started most of them in the first place.

435. Broadmindedness is highmindedness crushed by experience.

436. Here's a lesson to be garnered from an old sea captain's log:
The horn that's tooting loudest is the one that's in the fog.

437. Lord Chesterfield in his *Letters to His Son*:
Make other people like themselves a little better, my son, and I promise you they will like you very well.

438. According to the late Adlai Stevenson, the difference between a beautiful girl and a charming girl is that you notice the beauty, but the charmer notices you.

439. The man who wins all his arguments may lose most of his friends.

440. Senior (at football game): "See that big number 20 down there playing fullback? I think he's going to be our best man next year."

Coed: "But don't you think you ought to ask dad first?"

V

RELATING TO GOD
IN CHRIST

441. Water That Didn't Satisfy (John 4:7-29)

The battle of El Alamein had raged fiercely through the hours of the day when the heat was most intense on the sands of North Africa. When it seemed that the British had nearly reached the limits of their endurance, with an almost nonexistent water supply, they were suddenly surprised to see large numbers of the elite desert German army throw up their hands in surrender.

They came stumbling in, with parched, protruding tongues and thick, swollen lips, begging for water, even just a sip. What had happened was that as they overran the previous British position, there was a newly constructed water main there, and the German soldiers had shot holes in it and drank deeply.

However, the main was not in use for fresh water, and was being tested out by pumping seawater through it. What the Germans unwittingly drank was water from the Mediterranean Sea. The more they drank, the greater was their thirst in the battle. Thus was decided the issue of this crucial engagement.

Sea water might well be described as "earth water," retaining the elements that have for centuries washed into it.

— *Sunday School Times*

442. Pentecost may mean to many of us "plenty-of-cost," but is worth any price to get the power.   — Dwight L. Moody

443. "I Saved Nobody but Myself" (Esther 4:14; John 9:4)

A great story came out of the life of Dr. Gansaulas, the famous Chicago preacher of some years ago.

One Saturday morning as he was in his study writing a sermon, his nephew came in. This boy was a fine athlete about twenty-five years old, but he had never been quite able to find himself.

He noticed his uncle's sermon text, "For this cause I came into the world" (John 18:37). This is a statement of Jesus to Pilate.

The boy said, "Uncle, I wish I knew why I was born." That gave the preacher a chance to say a few words to him about life and soon the boy went out.

As the boy was walking on down the street he heard fire engines. The old Iroquois Theater was burning. In that fire more than five hundred people lost their lives. He rushed over and when he got there he saw a number of people at a balcony window.

Quickly he found a heavy plank, entered the building next to the theater and laid the plank across to the window. Then he stood in the window and helped many people across to safety. As he was working a heavy timber fell on him and knocked him to the pavement below. Just before he died his uncle reached him and said, "Now you know why you were born. You were born to save those people."

Several years later Dr. Gansaulas was traveling in Europe. One night he met a man in a hotel lobby and they were talking about several things. In the conversation the preacher happened to mention he was from Chicago and the other man suddenly became hysterical and began to mutter something over and over. Another man came and led him away.

Later, Dr. Gansaulas asked the third man what happened to the man he had been talking to. The man said it was a very sad case. He told him the man was in Chicago one Saturday and went to the old Iroquois Theater. The theater caught on fire but this man got out. To get out he had to climb over many screaming and fear-crazed people.

Though he himself was not harmed, he went crazy thinking about the experience. As a result, he says over and over, "I saved nobody but myself. I saved nobody but myself."

444. Getting a New Start (Isa. 58:12; Matt. 9:6)

A certain youth acquired quite a reputation as a "thorn in the flesh" of all his teachers. Because of his incorrigible behavior, teachers were getting more and more difficult to get for the thorn's class. Finally, a man was hired. Instead of "blowing his top," however, this man spoke with authority gentled by kindness and understanding. Under this kind of treatment the thorn's sharp point gradually began to dull. As the semester drew to an end, the change was hard to believe. No longer was he a problem, he was, instead, proving to be a scholar.

Then visitation night came. The parents were coming to examine their children's work, and this had the lad sweating. He was ashamed of that part of his work that evidenced his former lack of concern for his school work. He watched nervously as his parents picked up his notebook. As they turned the pages, complimentary comments were exchanged and smiles of approval were observed.

When his parents left the room the youth rushed to where his notebook lay. Picking it up, he quickly turned to where he knew the poor work was. But it wasn't there. His teacher had removed every page of the work his changed student was ashamed of.

445. Rom. 14:14-23; Heb. 12:1

When an athlete becomes a member of the football squad, he is put under training rules. There are certain foods that he is permitted to eat, whereas others are forbidden. Suppose I am entertaining a member of the football team. For dessert I serve a juicy piece of mince pie. I expect my guest to go for it eagerly, but he refuses it altogether. Why? Does he think it would be a sin to cut a bit of pie? No! Does he think the pie will kill him? No! He has been told that he might play the game better if he leaves off sweets. Therefore, he refuses the pie because he feels it his duty to be in the best form possible. This is perhaps the sanest test of what we may or may not do as Christians. There is no practice that is either right or wrong in itself. Shall I take this course or not? I can find help in my decision by asking this question: Will such a course help me to play the game or will it hinder? If it will help, I ought to take it; if it will hinder, I ought to reject it.

— Clovis Chappell, *Values That Last,* p. 45.
(By permission of Abingdon Press)

446. When you flee temptation, be sure you don't leave a forwarding address.

447. "Conscience," said an Indian, "is a three-cornered thing in my heart that stands still when I am good, but when I am bad, it turns around and the corners hurt a lot. If I keep on doing wrong, the corners wear off and it does not hurt any more."

448. Coach Gene Stallings of Texas A & M is refusing to speak at alumni meetings where beer is served. A man of strong Christian conviction, Coach Stallings' decision was quickly endorsed in the *Baptist Standard.* The weekly paper urged Baptists throughout the state to give Stallings their support.

449. Character is, for the most part, simply habit become fixed.
— Charles H. Parkhurst

450. The chains of habit are too weak to be felt till they are too strong to be broken.
— Samuel Johnson
Contributed by Miss Audree Lewis

451. Opportunity has to knock, but it is enough for temptation to stand outside and whistle.

452. Judg. 17:6; Rom. 13:14; Gal. 5:13; II Tim. 2:22

Question: I hear you [Billy Graham] talk on the radio about restricted sex. I believe in the playboy philosophy — that God made sex to enjoy, and he made man to be free. I believe that prudish people who say that something God created is dirty are to blame for the guilt that people carry.

Answer: First of all, I appreciate your frankness. But you are not the first frank person to be wrong. The playboy boasts of sex freedom. But you are smart enough to know that there is no freedom without a corresponding responsibility.

There is a Jewish legend about a leaf on a tree that wanted to be free — free to fly like a bird. He wiggled free from the branch he was attached to and went floating through the air. "I'm free, I'm free," he called to the other leaves. The next day when the sun came out he began to lose his color, and soon the life was oozing out of the leaf. He called to the other leaves, "Don't do as I have done. This is not freedom; it is death."

Life has many liberties but we are not free to do as we please. Ask the young man who took improper liberties with a girl, got her pregnant. He now has a wife he didn't want, and a child he didn't want, and a bad reputation besides. He is paying dearly for the liberty he sought and found.

453. "One of the basic characteristics of youth is curiosity. Jesus had been talked about a great deal by the adults. He had healed many. . . . Conflicting stories were circulated as to who He really was. Some reported that He was the promised Messiah. Others said, No. What could have been more exciting than to join the eager crowds that were always pressing Him? They would see for themselves. Surely the teen-agers were there. Nothing could have kept them away!"

— Gayle Ericson, 15, former student

454.   He went out one full-mooned night,
             Thought he'd paint the town.
             He had no trouble living it up,
             But plenty living it down!

455.   God's plan made a hopeful beginning;
             But man spoiled his chances by sinning
                 We trust that the story
                 Will end in God's glory,
             But at present, the other side's winning.

456. Within my earthly temple there's a crowd;
There's one of us that's humble, one that's proud;
There's one who's broken-hearted for sins;
There's one who unrepentant sits and grins;
There's one who loves his neighbor as himself;
There's one who cares for naught but fame and pelf.
From such perplexities I would be free,
If I could once determine which is me!

— Anonymous

457. The Boy and the Stinger (Job 19:4; James 4:3)
Somewhere I read of a spoiled child whose mother insisted that he must not be frustrated — that he must have whatever he wanted. The nurse understood. But one day the boy began a screaming demand while his nurse was restraining him at the window. His mother without investigation called from another room, "Let him have it." Just then he gave a scream of pain. The nurse called back, "He has it, ma'am — a bee."

So we can be sure that if we want some forbidden thing and even cry for it and get it perhaps unlawfully — we may find that it is a bee — not the honey kind for which we hoped but the stinger kind which nobody wants. What we want — often we get. But getting what we want we must take all that goes with it — if a bee, the stinger, too. — *Advocate*

458. Twenty-five Things We Can't Do (Matt. 12:34; Gal. 6:7)
1. Sow bad habits and reap a good character.
2. Sow jealousy and hatred and reap love and friendship.
3. Sow wicked thoughts and reap a clean life.
4. Sow wrong deeds and live righteously.
5. Sow crime and get away with it.
6. Sow dissipation and reap a healthy body.
7. Sow crooked dealings and succeed indefinitely.
8. Sow self-indulgence and not show it in your face.
9. Sow disloyalty and reap loyalty from others.
10. Sow dishonesty and reap integrity.
11. Sow profane words and reap clean speech.
12. Sow disrespect and reap respect.
13. Sow deception and reap confidence.
14. Sow intemperance and reap sobriety and temperance.
15. Sow untidiness and reap neatness.
16. Sow indifference and reap nature's rewards.
17. Sow mental or physical laziness and reap a responsible position in society.
18. Sow cruelty and reap kindness.
19. Sow wastefulness and reap thriftiness.

20. Sow cowardice and reap courage.

21. Sow destruction of other people's property and reap protection for your own.

22. Sow greed and envy and reap generosity.

23. Sow neglect of the Lord's House and reap strength in temptation.

24. Sow neglect of the Bible and reap a well-guided life.

25. Sow human thistles and reap human roses.

459. We should be as careful of the books we read as of the company we keep.

460. Limitations of the Clergy (Deut. 29:29; I Cor. 13:9)

The airliner flew into a violent thunderstorm and soon it was swaying and bumping around the sky. One very nervous lady happened to be sitting next to a clergyman and turned to him for comfort.

"Can't you do something?" she demanded forcefully.

"I'm sorry, madam," said the Reverend, gently. "I'm in sales, not management." —*Texas Outlook*

461. The Critic (I Cor. 4:7; II Cor. 3:5)

> A little seed lay in the ground
> And soon began to sprout.
> "Now, which of all the flowers around,"
> It mused "shall I come out?
>
> "The lily is so fair and proud,
> But just a trifle cold;
> The rose, I think, is rather loud,
> And then its fashion's old.
>
> "The violet — it is very well,
> But not a flower I'd choose,
> Nor yet the Canterbury bell —
> I never cared for blues."
>
> And so it criticized each flower.
> This supercilious seed,
> Until it woke one summer hour,
> And found itself a weed!
> —Anonymous

462. O Lord, never suffer us to think that we can stand by ourselves, and not need Thee. —John Donne

463. Our Need Is Our Claim (Ps. 40:17; Matt. 6:8; Phil. 4:19)

One day Dr. Barnardo of the Barnardo Orphan Home in

London was approached by a ragged little boy who asked admission into the orphanage. "But, my boy," said the doctor, "I do not know you. Who are you? What do you have to recommend you?"

The lad pointed to his ragged clothes, and said, "Sir, I thought these would be all I needed to recommend me." Dr. Barnardo caught the little fellow up into his arms — and took him in.

The sinner's *need* is his greatest claim on Christ. "We are all as an unclean thing, and all our righteousnesses are as filthy rags" (Isa. 64:6). "The Son of man is come to seek and to save that which was lost" (Luke 19:10).   —Clipped

464. Forgivers and Forgetfulness (I Cor. 14:20; I Peter 3:8)
>   Pity those guys
>   Who criticize
>   And minimize —
>   Theirs will be a great surprise
>   When those guys
>   Who don't criticize
>   But sympathize
>   Begin to rise
>   Above those guys
>   Who criticize!

                              —Anonymous

465. The deepest spring of action in us is the sight of action in another.   —William James

466. In Gethsemane there were four companies:
  I. The Lord alone — praying.
  II. The three disciples — sleeping
  III. The eight disciples — waiting.
  1V. The murderous mob — approaching.

The further from the Lord, the greater the crowd. Is this true today?

                              —*The Pentecostal Messenger*

467. When men speak ill of thee, live so that nobody will believe them.   —Plato

468. Let us so live that if someone proposed a monument to our memory no one would suggest brass as the most suitable material.

469. One never falls but on the side toward which one leans.

470. Precisely Put. Some years ago a man was complaining to his pastor about how the church was always asking for money.

"It's getting to be just one continuous give, give, give," he fumed. The preacher thought for a moment, then replied, "I want to thank you for one of the best definitions of Christianity I have ever heard."
—*El Paso Times*

471. Sow a thought, you reap an act
Sow an act, you reap a habit
Sow a habit, you reap a character
Sow a character, you reap a destiny.

472. A blind man is not helped by a mirror.

473. Slow Me Down, Lord (Isa. 30:18; James 1:4; Phil. 4:11)
"Slow me down, Lord!
Erase the pounding of my heart
By the quieting of my mind.
Steady my hurried pace
With a vision of the eternal reach of time.

Give me,
Amidst the confusion of my day,
The calmness of the everlasting hills.
Break the tensions of my nerves
With the soothing music of the singing streams
That live in my memory.

Help me to know
The magical restoring power of sleep.
Teach me the art
Of taking minute vacations of slowing down

to look at a flower;
to chat with an old friend or make a new one;
to play with a stray dog;
to watch a spider build a web;
to smile at a child;
or to read a few lines from a good book.

Remind me each day
That the race is not always to the swift;
That there is more to life than increasing its speed.

Let me look upward
Into the branches of the towering oak
And know that it grew great and strong
Because it grew slowly and well.

101

Slow me down, Lord,
And inspire me to send my roots deep
Into the soil of life's enduring values
That I may grow toward the stars
Of my greater destiny."

—O. L. Crain
Eastertime, 1957

474. Of the saddest words of tongue or pen,
The saddest are these: It might have been.

475. Jesus gave us the key of real life, life with a capital L, when He said, "I am come that they might have life, and that they might have it more abundantly" (John 10:10).

476. Great Spirit, help me
never to judge another
until I have walked
in his moccasins for two weeks.
—Sioux Indian Prayer

477. Let us have faith that right makes might. —Abraham Lincoln

478. Prov. 12:2; 13:5; 31:10, 30
Not all youth are compromising decent standards of dress. The 1959 Maid of Cotton, Malinda Diggs Berry, said, "I do not approve of displaying my body in front of the public." She was not belittling the other girls who paraded publicly in scanty attire. But she was committed to her stand that there was to be no cheesecake or bathing suit poses.

479. I Tim. 2:9; I Peter 3:3, 4
Indecent dress on the part of girls at John Marshall High in San Antonio, Texas, was brought to the attention of the principal, Homer Smith. One of the school's most highly respected Christian teachers approached him recently, complaining in this manner: "Mr. Smith, I am truly concerned about the short dresses worn by our girls. It's like this: Here's a little girl who sits down . . . her dress is so high. I try to face all my students . . . but it is embarrassing to me. I look down the other end of the row of chairs. But it's more of the same. . . ."
Principal Smith announced to the PTA that beginning the next Monday, John Marshall High would require girls with dresses of questionable length be sent to the counselor's office. "These," Smith said, "will be required to kneel. If the counselor finds the hem of her skirt does not touch the floor, then her dress will be considered too short and she'll be sent home to change."

At the conclusion of the meeting most of the parents came to wish Smith well and pledge their support.

480. Teen-agers Take a Stand

In Sturgeon Bay, Wisconsin, three teen-age girls refused last year to parade in bathing suits before judges and a public audience in the "Miss Wisconsin-Miss Universe" contest. The first to decline was the high school senior who had been crowned Cherry Blossom Queen. Her two maids of honor were then approached. But they firmly said they "didn't go for bathing suit parades either."

The press paid more attention to the ladylike stand of these three girls than it did to the winner of the beauty contest. Their courage of conviction taught a powerful lesson.

You, whoever you are, can do many things right now in a constructive way to restore decency to the marketplace. You can cleanse and purify the literary and entertainment fields. One person taking a courageous stand can have a telling effect.

The task of keeping modern life in the normal, healthy state which God expects of us as responsible human beings is a never ending job. If you persevere in reviving high standards of decency in all walks of life, you will make a Christlike contribution for everybody.

"Thou hast made man a little less than the angels, thou hast crowned him with honor; and hast set him over the works of thy hands" (Psalm 8:5, 6).

Help young people, O Lord, to stand up for decency.

—Father Keller, *Houston Post*

481. O God, help us to be masters of ourselves that we may be servants of others. —Sir Alec Paterson

482. O God, help us not to despise or oppose what we do not understand. —William Penn

483. All the world is an orphanage so long as its children know not God as their Father. —Martin Luther

484. You are either a missionary or you are a missionary field.
—*The Restorer*

485.
Thou art alive still,
While thy book does live
and we have
wits to read
and praise to give.
To the Memory of my beloved Master William Shakespeare
—Ben Jonson

103

486. Never be boastful; someone may come along who knew you as a child. —Chinese Proverb

487. *Self-respect* cannot be hunted. It cannot be purchased. It is never for sale. It cannot be fabricated out of public relations. It comes to us when we are alone, in quiet moments, in quiet places, when we suddenly realize that, knowing the good, we have done it; knowing the beautiful, we have served it; knowing the truth, we have spoken it. —A. Whitney Criswold, in a speech

488. Regular Church Attendance Is Important: Remember the banana — every time it leaves the bunch it gets skinned.

489. Prov. 5:22; 26:27; Rom. 14:13

At the close of the high school commencement service a young girl and her boy friend who had just graduated went out to celebrate. At midnight the girl's father was awakened by a phone call. He was urged to the scene of an accident.

When he arrived he found the dead body of his daughter lying in a ditch and the body of her boy friend in the wreckage. On the pavement lay a broken bottle of whiskey. The smell of liquor was all around.

In his desperation the father cried, "If I could only get my hands on the criminal who sold them the bottle!"

He went home and being totally unnerved, went to his liquor cabinet for a drink. His bottle was gone and in its place he found a note which read: "Daddy, we wanted to celebrate so we borrowed your bottle. I am sure you won't mind." This father had provided the death bottle for his own daughter.

This tragic story is true. It is not an isolated account though. The very same thing is happening in our little town.

The blame for teen-age drinking can not be placed on one group. Teen-agers, whether they be students or ex-students; adults, whether they be parent, teachers, or friends, share the blame, or if you would like the kinder word, responsibility, for teen-age drinking. —*Longhorn Newspaper*

490. One pastor said that his church would be the first church to go up in the rapture. He gave his reason: The Bible said "The dead in Christ shall rise first."

491. Prov. 20:1; Eph. 5:18

Of a total of five million alcoholics in this country, approximately one-fifth are women. Alcoholism costs the American public more than $1,000,000,000 per year, is responsible for more than one-quarter of the nonsupport cases in Chicago, more than 85 percent of the first admissions to state hospitals in New York. More than half the fatal traffic accidents in America are caused by drunk drivers. As a public health problem alcoholism now ranks fourth in the United States, behind heart disease, cancer and mental illness.

492. A wise man does not put his eye to a wasps' nest to see if they are at home. —American Indian Proverb

493. I Cor. 7:32

Now I lay me down to sleep,
The sermon is long and Oh, so deep,
But if he should quit before I awake,
Be sure and wake me, for goodness' sake!

494. Phil. 4:8

The University of New Mexico's athletic department was having difficulty keeping their athletic supplies, particularly sweat shirts, marked with the university's name. To diminish the status symbol appeal of the sweat shirts, someone came up with the solution of marking shirts:

The University of New Mexico
Athletic Department
Third String

495. Rom. 12:1; Eph. 5:20

Music has often been a manifestation of faith. No one proved it more than did Fritz Kreisler with his long and dedicated career to both music and faith.

One of the greatest of violinists, Kreisler won the Grand Prix at the age of twelve from the Conservatory in Vienna. In 1889 he made his first successful tour of the United States. From that time on he thrilled and inspired millions with his interpretations and his own compositions. He once said, "I have never opened my violin case, I have never touched a bow in my life without offering them as a gift back to God."

On his eighty-fifth birthday he declared his durability was a "present from God." When he died a year later he left the world richer in faith as well as beauty through his music.

496. Do the Ends Justify the Means? (Ps. 27:14)

The temptation to use questionable means in order to achieve a good objective is often a strong one. But you will overcome all such enticements if you are motivated by a sincere desire to honor God, respect the rights of others and be true to yourself.

497. There is no right way to do a wrong thing.

498. Watch It! (Prov. 1:4; 26:12)

If you need a good story that illustrates how to put someone in his place, tell about the young Hercules-type who was bragging about his strength, about the remarkable athletic feats he had accomplished.

"Tell you what," a wan old-timer said. "I'll bet you ten bucks I can move a load in a wheelbarrow that you can't wheel back."

The strong man agreed with a smile, and at length a wheelbarrow was found.

"OK", the old man told the youth. "Get in."   *Houston Post*

499. Temptation (I Cor. 10:13; James 1:12)

A favorite illustration of Dr. Charles L. Allen is the one about the dog who had been trained to obey his master under every circumstance. The supreme test for the dog was when he would be very hungry, the master would put on the floor before him a tempting piece of meat but then command, "Do not eat." The dog's mouth would literally water. He would tremble as the odor filled his nostrils.

How could the dog refrain from eating? Instead of looking at the meat, he gazed steadily into the eyes of his master. In so doing the dog had the strength to resist the temptation not to obey the command.   There is a wonderful little chorus which says, "Turn your eyes upon Jesus, look full in His wonderful face." When one keeps before him the face of the Lord, he has strength he can use with much effectiveness.

500. Father Loses Life to Save His Son (John 3:16)

A father who threw himself into a sewer trench cave-in to save his son accomplished his purpose. The boy was on the road to recovery Thursday. But the father is dead.

Lehi contractor Darrel Adams, thirty-nine, was standing by the trench watching his seventeen-year-old son Richard at work in the eight-foot deep slit. The father saw a heavy, wet section of the trench-side slip and he jumped between it and his boy, covering the youth.

The tremendous weight crushed the life from the father in a minute or so, but not before he told an employee to call the Lehi volunteer fire department.

Firemen got Richard out and sent him to a hospital with little more than contusions. They tried mouth-to-mouth resuscitation on the father, but it failed.

Assistant Fire Chief Ned Wilson said only the father's head and hand were above the dirt when the firemen arrived.

Wilson added:

"We got the boy uncovered a little bit and he asked us to forget him and get his dad out. He said, 'Do you know where he's hurt?'

"There wasn't any use working on the father. A mortician said the dad didn't know what hit him. But he must have been alive a minute, or two, because he told his helper to call the fire department.

"I'm sure the boy would have died also. It looked like the father jumped in purposely to take the weight.

"We told the boy we'd have him out in a few minutes. He said he thought he was going to die, and if he could take that, he could wait a few minutes while we helped his father."

501. Captain Paul Landsdowne of the Long Beach Police Juvenile Division estimates that crime costs America $20,000,000,000 a year, $10,000,000 of which is accounted for by juveniles.

502. Hell (Matt. 25:46)
"Nobody believes in hell anymore. . . . You may want to argue the question philosophically, but I tell you it is one of those things that keep us on the right track, and we don't have half enough things to keep us on the right track!"
—Superior Court Judge Fred Miller

503. Getting a New Start
God's forgiveness tears the shameful pages from the notebook of our life and gives us a new start in life.

504. Science and Religion (Eccles. 7:25; Dan. 1:4)
There can be no conflict between science and religion. Science is a reliable method of finding truth. Religion is the search for a satisfying way of life. Science is growing; yet a world that has science needs, as never before, the inspiration that religion offers.
—Arthur H. Compton, Physicist

505. The probability of life originating from accident is comparable to the probability of the unabridged dictionary resulting from an explosion in a printing shop.
—Edwin Conklin, Biologist

506. I believe in an immortal soul. Science has proved that nothing disintegrates into nothingness. Life and soul, therefore, cannot disintegrate into nothingness, and so are immortal.
—Wernher von Braun,
Missile Expert

507. The man who regards his own life and that of his fellow creatures as meaningless is not merely unfortunate but almost disqualified for life.

—Albert Einstein,
Theoretical Physicist

508. Christ has suffered for our sins. He has paid the penalty for us, so that there is therefore no condemnation to them that are in Christ Jesus. He has, with his own blood, written "paid" across the ledgers of Heaven. —Peter Marshall

509. If there be anything in my style of thought to be commended, the credit is due to my kind parents in instilling into my mind an early love of the Scripture. —Daniel Webster

510. "Don't try to mend a burst soap bubble."

511. "The thief shouts loudest when something is stolen from him."

512. "The Devil is not so dangerous when he comes as a roaring lion as when he comes as a wagging dog."

513. At twenty-five years of age, so statistics show:
  One in 5,000 becomes a Christian
  At thirty-five, one in 25,000
  At fifty, one in 150,000
  At seventy-five, an unconverted person is almost certainly doomed eternally.
  Likewise, 78 per cent of the decisions made for Christ are made between the ages of ten and sixteen.
  Therefore — win for Christ in grammar school — secure life decisions in high school.

—*Successful Sunday School Teaching*
By Dorothy C. Haskin

514. Matt. 24:14; Mark 16:15
  "We have with us this morning a living demonstration of the work of missions," the minister said, introducing the convert from Hinduism. "Our speaker is a Christian gentleman, converted from paganism, a product of our missionary enterprise."
  The speaker from India arose, smiled faintly at the congregation and replied, "Your pastor is a more conspicuous demonstration of missionary achievement than I. Centuries ago when my fathers were already a civilized people, writing the philosophies of ancient India, his fathers and yours were barbarians drinking wine from

human skulls, the terror of the ancient world. When I see what
the Gospel has done for Anglo-Saxons, I am persuaded of its re-
deeming power."   —Clipped

515. He who has the Holy Spirit in his heart and the Scripture
in his hands has all he needs.   —Alexander Maclaren

516. Deut. 20:8; Rom. 14:7; I Tim. 4:12
My Influence
My life shall touch a dozen lives before this day is done,
    Leave countless marks for good or ill ere sets the evening sun,
This is the wish I always wish, the prayer I always pray;
    Lord, may my life help other lives it touches by the way.
                                                    —Selected

517. The humblest individual exerts some influence, either for
good or evil, upon others.   —Henry Ward Beecher

518.   O what a tangled web we weave,
                When first we practice to deceive.
                                          —Sir Walter Scott

519. The doors of opportunity are marked "push."

520. I have known God to use people who never had a chance,
but I have never known God to use a person who has had a
chance and will not take it.   —Bob Jones, Sr.

521.   The stairs of opportunity
                        Are sometimes hard to climb;
                And that can only be well done
                        By one step at a time.
                But he who would go to the top
                        Ne'er sits down and despairs;
                Instead of staring up the steps
                        He just steps up the stairs.
                                          —Author Unknown

522. "It Is Christ or Nothing" (Acts 4:12)
    I find both [East and West] in the same human need.
The soul of modern man is empty — in East and West — and he
cannot stand this emptiness, meaninglessness, purposelessness. So
he is unhappy and frustrated.
    We don't have to speak against Hinduism, Buddhism or
Mohammedanism, we have to speak against the emptiness in man.
    As far as I can see, there is no alternative to Jesus Christ in

filling that emptiness. There is nobody else seriously on the field. It is Christ or nothing. —E. Stanley Jones

523. As you took forgiveness from the hand of the dying Christ, take your share of the Pentecostal gift from the hand of the living Christ. —F. B. Meyer

524. "Top Teens' Tactics" — In Church (Ps. 101:2; II Thess. 3:7)
1. Reverence God and His house at all times.
2. Treat song books, pews and all church property with top respect and consideration. (You're being watched from above.)
3. Refuse to talk and move around unnecessarily in church.
4. Treat all teen-age visitors as you would like to be treated if you were in their place.
5. Invite your unsaved friends to the altar when the invitation is given.
6. Keep your relationship with the opposite sex on a Christian level by
    a. sticking to a "hands off" policy.
    b. being courteous at all times.
7. Dress to please Christ, not to attract the attention of others. Whatever your best is, wear it to church. (You are an ambassador of the King of Glory!)

525.   He who has never called the traitor to a stand;
    Nor ever turned that he a wrong might right;
    He has no enemies to stay his hand;
    For he has been a coward in the right.
                    —Anonymous

526. The flower of youth never appears more beautiful than when it bends toward the sun of righteousness.
                    —Matthew Henry

527. I sank away from Thee, and I wandered, O my God,
    Too much astray from Thee my stay, in these days of my youth,
    And I became to myself a barren land.
                —Augustine, *Confession*

528. Ten Ways to Be Unhappy (John 6:63; Phil. 2:5)
1. To forget the many good things in life you have and to overemphasize the few things you lack.
2. To think that money is more important than it actually is.
3. To think that you are indispensable.
4. To think that you have too much to do.
5. To think that you are exceptional, or entitled to special privileges.

6. To forget that a sense of responsibility is essential to a democratic society.

7. To think that you can control your automatic nervous system by reason or will.

8. To forget others.

9. To cultivate a pessimistic outlook.

10. To feel sorry for yourself — perhaps the worst mental habit.

—C. H. Baylor, *Sunshine*

529. $1,400,000 Per Hour for Liquor

(AP) — The treasurer of the Women's Christian Temperance Union has said that Americans are spending a record $1,484,018 an hour on liquor, wine, and beer.

The treasurer, Mrs. H. F. Powell of Evanston, Illinois, said:

"Americans are nightly indulging in the greatest drinking bouts in history. Were the drunks that stagger under the cloak of early-morning darkness to emerge in daylight, an aroused public would demand a return to prohibition at once."

530. God grant me
The serenity to accept the things I cannot change,
The courage to change the things I can,
And the wisdom to know the difference.

531. Here are seven suggestions as to how you might make up your mind next time you're not sure.

1. Ask yourself, would Christ do this?

2. Find a situation similar to yours in the Bible and see how it was handled.

3. Talk it over with your parents.

4. Counsel with your pastor or Sunday School teacher.

5. Read a good book on the subject.

6. Can you apply Colossians 3:23 to it?

7. Finally, as someone has wisely put it, if you're not sure — don't!

532. Acts 4:3

The story is told of a weary traveler who was passing along a lonely roadway and noticed in his path a dry, shrivelled leaf. Picking it up, he was amazed at the lovely perfume it exuded.

"Oh, you poor withered leaf," he exclaimed, "whence comes this exquisite perfume?"

The leaf replied, "I have lain for a long time in the company of a rose."

533. Ability Plus (II Sam. 18:3; Isa. 6:8; II Tim. 2:21)

Ability alone will not make you successful in the Master's

Service. Not what you have, but what you *do* with what you have will determine your future usefulness. Your ability shows what you can do, but the following characteristics will show them what you *are*:

Availability — Are you available for service — any kind? Don't worry. God will never call you to do anything unless He has given you the ability to do it with. But to be unusually used of God, be unusually available.

Reliability — Can you be depended upon to do the job, and do it right?

> If a task is once begun,
> Never leave it till it's done
> Be the labor great or small,
> Do it well or not at all.
>
> —Anonymous

Durability — How long can you be depended upon? Do you last only as long as the praise and attention do? When the going gets tough, the tough get going! When things get dark some like to quit. But did you ever notice that it's not until darkness falls that the stars come out?

Excitability — How enthusiastic are you? Make your enthusiasm not like a neon light that goes on and off, but rather like the sun — it shines constantly, whether people see it or not.

534. If I Say No to Temptation

> When others say yes to temptation,
> God help me to say no.
> When others fall because of deeds unjust
> In thee O God I'll put my trust.
> If close to thee I walk each day
> O God that always I'll trust and obey
> I'll shout victory, victory on that great day
> I said no to temptation and God made the way.
>
> —Unknown

535. It is not a question of who or what you are, but whether God controls you.   —J. Wilbur Chapman

536. Conscience (John 8:9; I Tim. 1:5)

> I can never hide myself from me;
> I see what others may never see;
> I know what others may never know;
> I never can fool myself, and so,
> Whatever happens, I want to be
> Self-respecting and conscience free.
>
> —Edgar A. Guest

537. Some baseball teams — and a lot of golfers — have the same weakness. They stand too close to the ball after they hit it.

538. Prov. 29:16; Micah 13:13; I Thess. 5:21

I'm sure there's no good reason why
I can't see in my ear with my eye;
I believe I can do it
If I put my mind to it —
You never can tell till you try.

539. A teen-ager in Michigan amputated his own leg with a jack-knife when it got entangled in a farm machine.

The seventeen-year-old lad was trying to fix the corn-picking machine he had been operating when the vehicle suddenly lurched. Both his left foot and left hand were trapped and he was in danger of bleeding to death.

Reaching for his knife with his right hand, he cut off the leg just below the knee. Then he pulled his other hand free and crawled 125 yards to a tractor and drove to the nearest house.

The brave young man found no one home, so he phoned his mother, who had an ambulance sent to pick him up.

People rightly go to great lengths, even to the point of cutting off a limb, in order to save the life of the body. How much more, then, should any of us do to avoid spiritual death?

Just as the body is subject to the soul, so too should each of us prefer death rather than to commit even one grave offense against God's law.

"If your hand or your foot is an occasion of sin to you, cut it off and cast it from you!" (Matt. 18:8).

Let me prepare now, O Lord, for the trials of life that are sure to come my way.   —Father Keller, *Houston Post*

540. Inscribed over the fireplace of the Hind's Head Hotel in Bray-on-Thames, not far from London, are these words: FEAR KNOCKED AT THE DOOR. FAITH ANSWERED. NO ONE WAS THERE.

541. Why Young People Drop Out of Church

This is the result of a poll conducted in two thousand churches of twenty-five evangelical denominations and a number of independent churches in all fifty states by Youth and Research Commissions of the National Sunday School Association.

Eighty per cent of these churches reported a high number of drop-outs, and the age that is more fatal to teens than any other is sixteen. Sixty per cent of the deserters left churches of one hundred fifty or less members. Fifty-six per cent of the dropouts were professed Christians; and one out of three were unsaved. (Consider ⅓ of your church's youth in hell.) Sixty-two per cent of these drop-outs were regular attenders until they left the church. As to sex, the boys have a slight edge on the number of drop-outs or about 52 per cent. Forty-nine per cent of these drop-outs started attending church before they were *six* years old. (This would indicate that the leaders of the children may have failed to plant the real desire to attend church in their heart.)

In each church the pastor gave a questionnaire to two of the young people who had left the church. They were to list the reasons that caused them to forsake church. The pastors were also asked to fill out a questionnaire and list the reasons why they thought the teens had left.

Here is the list that the teen-agers gave, giving the top eight reasons in order that caused them to leave:

1. There are not enough youth activities at the church. This was ranked No. 12 by the pastors.

2. Adults in the church are hypocrites.

An eighteen-year-old Minnesota girl wrote, "There were too many people who were so 'holy' on Sunday, but the rest of the week you would never know that they ever went to church." The pastors ranked this No. 4.

3. Church is boring.

The irrelevance and boredom of church activities are of great concern to many youth. One high school graduate reported that the sermons ·and lessons did not speak to her or her needs. Interestingly, pastors rated this item as No. 13.

4. Too many other conflicting activities.

Pastors rated this almost the same — No. 3.

5. Parents didn't encourage me. (As a Minnesota boy wrote, "I just quit going. It was easy to stay at home because my parents did not attend." Pastors view this as *No. 1.*

6. Didn't care about religious things.

Here's what drop-outs prefer instead of church: to sleep in, sports, dancing, social activities, cars, running around with buddies, school activities, girls, shows. Pastors rated this item No. 2.

7. Too much schoolwork and school activities. Pastors rated this about the same — No. 6.

8. Friends not at church.

Young people are not interested in attending church if their friends don't go there. Apparently, pastors, who rated this item very low (No. 18), are not alert to the importance that teens place on friendships. Young people find "social security" in being with the gang. Loyalty to friends runs high.

Other drop-out reasons given by the teens are: broke up

with my boyfriend (or girlfriend), preferred to watch TV, disagreed with the church's beliefs, kids at church were unfriendly, was pressured to attend, was embarrassed (by being asked to pray in public, by not knowing the Bible, etc.), friends kidded me for going, just neglected to go, had no transportation, etc.

In comparing the two lists, the teens blamed the churches and the people, while the pastors blamed the parents and the teens themselves.

When asked what agencies in the church most dissatisfied them, the drop-outs listed Sunday School the highest and camp the lowest. Church services were second and youth meetings were third.

The pastors ranked prayer meetings as highest; however, not enough young people attend them to know enough about them to dislike them. The pastors thought the Sunday School would be fairly well liked.

Most teens said that the Sunday Schools were dry and uninteresting, while the preacher preached to the adults only, in the church services. It was often complained that the lesson or sermons were not dealing with current or real problems of living. Twenty-eight and eight-tenths per cent of the young people who discussed the youth meetings said that the meetings were unplanned or disorderly. Other "gripes" were: uninteresting subjects (26.6 per cent), had poor leadership (15.5 per cent), lacked variety (15.5 per cent), and included no serious study of the Bible (13.3 per cent).

What Can Be Done?

1. More youth activities.

The youth said that they wanted such activities as sports, socials and outings, pastors' instruction classes, camps, banquets, and weekday clubs. They ask to be allowed to serve and be more a part of the church. They wanted to fulfill such duties as Sunday School class secretaries, ushers, songleaders, sing in the choir, go on gospel teams to jails and old folks' homes, attend youth conferences and so forth at other churches, etc.

2. Challenging Sunday School lessons.

Make each Sunday morning's session a real brain-tickler and a soul blesser. Make the study of God's Word an exciting, appealing adventure.

3. Sharp youth meetings.

See that youth programs are well planned. Make them youth-centered, not sponsor-centered. Make the program to deal with one of the subjects that holds the interest of the youth. Programs on Christian life, dating and marriage, witnessing, beliefs of people in cults and false religions, knowing God's will, etc., are what they wanted.

4. Sermons that appeal to teens.

Young people want pastors to think of them as part of the congregation, and not preach exclusively to the adults. Messages from God's Word, delivered with a vocabulary and in a fashion that young people can grasp, are in top demand.

5. Well-qualified youth leaders.

The drop-outs were looking for adult leaders who were understanding and who were genuinely interested in youth and would spend time with them.

6. Strong church-parent ties.

Instruct the parents of the teens on youth characteristics, and inform the parents what the church is doing for the youth. Don't try to take the place of the parents, but get the parents behind you in your programs.
— Compiled by Roy B. Zuck, *Eternity*—May, 1963
Condensed by Woodvall Moore

542. Truth does not hurt unless it should.

543. True gold fears not the fire.

544. Water can both sustain and engulf a ship.

545. He who soars not, suffers not by a fall.

546. To pretend to satisfy one's desires by possessions is like putting out a fire with straw.

547. Without Wax

In ancient days, contractors in the Roman Empire often were required to insert a clause in their contracts, to effect that a particular building was to be constructed "without wax." Stones sometimes were broken or sheared off in being transported, and unscrupulous contractors filled in with wax to conceal the defect. Before long, the weather destroyed the wax, leaving the flaw exposed.

We are challenged to construct our lives "without wax," so it will not be necessary to conceal defects with the wax of deceit and pretense.

A famous sculptor had almost completed his masterpiece when he discovered a minor flaw on the back of his human figures. For days he worked carefully to remove the blemish, until finally one of his apprentices remarked to him: "Master, your sculptured group will stand so near the wall that no one can ever see that defect, so why do you work so carefully to remove it?"

"My son, God will see it," the artist replied.

God knows about the flaws in our lives which may be imperceptible to our fellows; and He knows where we are using wax to conceal the shabbiness of our living.

"Character is what you are in the dark," said Dwight L. Moody. It behooves us to strive to build our structure of life in such a careful manner that wax will not be necessary to cover the blemishes. — Leo Bennett

548. II Sam. 18:5; James 2:22
A teen-age boy signed up as a trumpeter in the school band. After a few fearful noises from the horn, the band teacher demanded, "Why didn't you tell me you couldn't play the trumpet?" "How did I know," replied the youth. "I never tried before!"
— Contributed by Luke E. Hollandsworth

549. Beliefs are not the same as convictions. As R. D. Heard puts it, "Beliefs are what a man holds; convictions, what holds the man!"

550. Prov. 14:9; Isa. 59:2; I John 1:7
God promised to save you from sin, but first you must really understand what sin is. Sin is a refusal to live intelligently or to conform our lives to the truth of God's Word. It is *not* just a weakness, but a state of rebellion. You do not sin because you don't understand — but because you refuse to recognize your *very clear* obligations to God and man. Now God has honestly promised you mercy, pardon, peace and happiness — but only on *His* terms.

Without Christ you have a crippled conscience. The Apostle Paul described it as a ". . . mind and conscience that is defiled . . ." (Titus 1:15).

Yes — without Christ, you are a rebel and you don't deserve pity. You have a will and can be held accountable for your own sin. There is no such thing as a "helpless sinner." You are not responsible for the sin of Adam and Eve — you are responsible for your own. The gospel is bad news to those who live for self and good news only to those who surrender intelligently.
— Adapted from *The Cross and the Switchblade*

551. Ezek. 7:23; Matt. 15:19, 20
The moral state of our youth today is at the lowest ebb in history. There are now over one million abortions in the United States each year. One out of six American brides is pregnant when she marries. Two hundred fifty thousand illegitimate children are born every year. The cost to our government to aid dependent children totals over $180 million each year. Then add to this the 18 per cent increase in the national crime rate —

thousands of new goof ball addicts, teen-age alcoholics, reckless hot-rodding, beach riots and disrespect for law and order.

— The Cross and the Switchblade

552. Predicting Juvenile Delinquency

Cambridge, Mass. — Children who are likely to become juvenile delinquents may be spotted when only two or three years old, according to a noted scientist, Dr. Eleanor Tuoroff Glueck of Harvard University. After years of studying infant and family characteristics, Dr. Glueck and her husband, Sheldon, developed a table for determining whether a child may turn out to be a juvenile delinquent. The table lists five important factors: 1. Undesirable characteristics in parents, such as alcoholism, criminal tendencies, and emotional disturbances; 2. The degree of parents' affection for the child; 3. The degree of a child's restlessness; 4. Destructiveness; and 5. Resistance to authority.

Two years ago, the New York City Board reported on a ten-year study in which an earlier version of the table was used for determining the juvenile deliquency potential of five-and-one-half to six-year-old children. The Board found that of thirty-three boys who were identified as having a high delinquency potential when they entered first grade, twenty-five became persistent lawbreakers before the age of seventeen.

— Current Science, January 19, 1966

553. Christ

Christ is all sufficient. For the

ARTIST He is the altogether lovely, Song of Solomon 5:16

ARCHITECT He is the chief cornerstone, I Peter 2:6

ASTRONOMER He is the sun of righteousness, Malachi 4:2

BAKER He is the living bread, John 6:51

BANKER He is the unsearchable riches, Ephesians 3:8

BUILDER He is the sure foundation, Isaiah 28:16; I Corinthians 3:11

CARPENTER He is the door, John 10:9

EDITOR He is the good tidings of great joy, Luke 2:10

ELECTRICIAN He is the light of the world, John 8:12

FARMER He is the sower and the Lord of the harvest, Matthew 13:37; Luke 10:2

FLORIST He is the rose of Sharon and the lily of the valley, Song of Solomon 2:1

JEWELER He is the living precious stone, I Peter 2:4

LAWYER He is the counselor, lawgiver and advocate, Isaiah 9:6; I John 2:1

LABORER He is the giver of rest, Matthew 11:28

— Clipped

554. What Is Jesus Christ to You?

To the ARTIST He is the ONE ALTOGETHER LOVELY

To the ARCHITECT He is the CHIEF CORNERSTONE

To the BAKER He is the LIVING BREAD

To the BANKER He is the HIDDEN TREASURE

To the BIOLOGIST He is the LIFE

To the BUILDER He is the SURE FOUNDATION

To the DOCTOR He is the GREAT PHYSICIAN

To the EDUCATOR He is the GREAT TEACHER

To the FARMER He is the LORD OF THE HARVEST

To the FLORIST He is the ROSE OF SHARON, the LILY OF THE VALLEY

To the GEOLOGIST He is the ROCK OF AGES

To the JURIST He is the RIGHTEOUS JUDGE

To the JEWELER He is the PEARL OF GREAT PRICE

To the LAWYER He is the COUNSELOR, LAWGIVER and ADVOCATE

To the HORTICULTURIST He is the TRUE VINE

To the NEWSPAPER MAN He is GOOD TIDINGS OF GREAT JOY

To the OCULIST He is the LIGHT OF THE WORLD

To the PHILANTHROPIST He is the UNSPEAKABLE GIFT

To the PHILOSOPHER He is the WISDOM OF GOD

To the PREACHER He is the WISDOM OF GOD

To the SCULPTOR He is the LIVING STONE

To the SERVANT He is the GOOD MASTER

To the STATESMAN He is the DESIRED OF ALL NATIONS

To the STUDENT He is the INCARNATE TRUTH

To the THEOLOGIAN He is the AUTHOR AND FINISHER OF OUR FAITH

To the TRAVELER He is the NEW AND LIVING WAY

To the TOILER He is the GIVER OF REST

To the SINNER He is the LAMB OF GOD that taketh away the sin of the world.

To the CHRISTIAN He is the SON OF THE LIVING GOD — SAVIOUR, REDEEMER AND LORD.

— Clipped

VI

PLANNING FOR
THE FUTURE

555. I Have Found Today (Ps. 118:24; II Cor. 2:6)

I've shut the door on yesterday,
　　Its sorrows and mistakes;
I've locked within its gloomy walls
　　Past failures and heartaches
And now I throw the key away
　　To seek another room,
And furnish it with hope and smiles
　　And every springtime bloom.

No thought shall enter this abode
　　That has a hint of pain,
And worry, malice and distrust
　　Shall never therein reign.
I've shut the door on yesterday
　　And thrown the key away —
Tomorrow holds no doubt for me,
　　Since I have found today.
　　　　　　　　　　— Anonymous

556. II Sam. 10:12; Ps. 33:12

I Speak for Democracy was written by Elizabeth Ellen Evans, a sixteen-year-old high school student of Akron, Ohio. This eloquent essay won a national contest sponsored by the United States Junior Chamber of Commerce. It has been reproduced many times since it was read over the radio-TV program, "Voice of Firestone."

I am an American.
Listen to my words, Fascist, Communist.
Listen well, for my country is a strong country, and my
　　message is a strong message.
I am an American, and I speak for democracy.
My ancestors have left their blood
　　on the green at Lexington and the snow at Valley Forge,
　　on the walls at Fort Sumter and the fields at Gettysburg,
　　on the waters of the River Marne and in the shadows of
　　　　the Argonne Forest,

on the beachheads of Salerno and Normandy and the
sands of Okinawa,

on the bare, bleak hills called Pork Chop and Old Baldy
and Heartbreak Ridge.

A million and more of my countrymen have died for freedom.
My country is their eternal monument.

They live on

in the laughter of a small boy as he watches a circus
clown's antics.

in the sweet, delicious coldness of the first bite of pepper-
mint ice cream on the Fourth of July,

in the tenseness of a baseball crowd as the umpire calls
"Batter Up!"

in the high school band's rendition of "Stars and Stripes
Forever" in the Memorial Day parade.

in the clear sharp ring of a school bell on a fall morning
and

in the triumph of a six-year-old as he reads aloud for
the first time.

They live on

in the eyes of an Ohio farmer surveying his acres of corn
and potatoes and pastures,

in the brilliant gold of hundreds of acres of wheat stretching across the flat miles of Kansas,

in the milling of cattle in the stockyards of Chicago,

in the precision of an assembly line in an automobile
factory in Detroit,

in the perpetual glow of the nocturnal skylines of Pitts-
burgh and Birmingham and Gary.

They live on

in the voice of a young Jewish boy saying the sacred
words from the Torah:

"Hear, O Israel, the Lord our God, the Lord is One. Thou
shalt love the Lord thy God with all thy heart and
with all thy soul and with all thy might,"

and in the voice of a Catholic girl praying: "Hail, Mary,
full of grace, the Lord is with thee"

and the voice of a Protestant boy singing: "A mighty
Fortress is our God, a Bulwark never failing. . . ."

An American named Carl Sandburg wrote these words:

"I know a Jew fishcrier down on Maxwell Street with a
voice like a north wind blowing over corn stubble in January. He dangles herring before prospective customers
evincing a joy identical with that of Pavlova dancing. His
face is that of a man terribly glad to be selling fish, terribly

glad that God made fish, and customers to whom he may call his wares from a pushcart."

There is a voice in the soul of every human being that cries out to be free.

America has answered that voice.

America has offered freedom and opportunity, such as no land before her has ever known, to a Jewish fishcrier down on Maxwell Street with the face of a man terribly glad to be selling fish.

She has given him the right to own his own pushcart, to sell his herring on Maxwell Street.

She has given him an education for his children, and a tremendous faith in the nation that has made these things his.

Multiply that fishcrier by 180,000,000 — 180,000,000 mechanics and farmers and housewives and coal miners and truck drivers and chemists and lawyers and plumbers and priests — all glad, terribly glad to be what they are, terribly glad to be free to work and eat and sleep and speak and love and pray and live as they desire, as they believe!

And those 180,000,000 Americans — those 180,000,000 free Americans — have

more roast beef and mashed potatoes, the yield of American labor and land,

more automobiles and telephones,

more safety razors and bathtubs,

more orlon sweaters and aureomycin, the fruits of American initiative and enterprise,

more public schools and life insurance policies, symbols of American security and faith in the future,

more laughter and song than any other people on earth!

This is my answer, Fascist, Communist!

Show me a country greater than our country.

Show me a people more energetic, creative, progressive, bigger-hearted and happier than our people.

Not until then will I consider your way of life.

For I am an American, and I speak for democracy.

557. In order that people may be happy in their work, these three things are needed: they must be fit for it; they must not do too much of it, and they must have a sense of success in it.

— Ruskin

558. To recognize a mistake is quite simple, because most of us are surrounded by people who will gladly point out our errors.

The ability to accept the responsibility for things that go wrong is a quality that separates the men from the boys. The most unusual phrase in the English language is *"I am at fault — I am to blame."*

Learning from a mistake is what is known in business circles as turning a liability into an asset. A mistake can be valuable if it contributes something to our education. — *New Jersey P-T*

559. I would rather have you day by day fix your eyes upon the greatness of your country, until you become filled with the love of her, and when you are impressed by the spectacle of her glory, reflect that it has been acquired by men who knew their duty and had the courage to do it. — Pericles

560. A nation with no regard for its past will have little future worth remembering. — Blake Clark

561. I Am the United States

I was born on July 4, 1776, and the Declaration of Independence is my birth certificate. The bloodlines of the world run in my veins, because I offered freedom to the oppressed. I am the United States.

I am 185,000,000 living souls, and the ghost of millions who have lived and died for me.

I am Nathan Hale and Paul Revere. I stood at Lexington and fired the shot heard around the world. I am Washington, Jefferson, and Patrick Henry. I am John Paul Jones, the Green Mountain boys, and Davy Crockett. I am Lee, Grant, and Abe Lincoln.

I am the Brooklyn Bridge, the wheat lands of Kansas, and the granite hills of Vermont. I am the coal fields of the Virginias and Pennsylvania; the fertile lands of the West; the Golden Gate and the Grand Canyon. I am Independence Hall, the Monitor and the Merrimac.

I am big. I sprawl from the Atlantic to the Pacific, three million square miles throbbing with industry. I am more than 5,000,000 farms; I am forest, field, mountain and desert. I am quiet villages . . . and cities that never sleep. You can look at me and see Ben Franklin walking down the streets of Philadelphia with his bread loaf under his arm. You can see Betsy Ross with her needle. You can see the lights of Christmas, and hear the strains of "Auld Lang Syne" as the calendar turns.

I am Babe Ruth and the World Series. I am 169,000 schools and colleges and 250,000 churches where people worship God as they think best. I am a ballot dropped in a box, the roar of a crowd in a stadium, and the voice of a choir in a cathedral. I am an editorial in a newspaper, and a letter to a Congressman.

I am Eli Whitney and Stephen Foster. I am Tom Edison,

Albert Einstein, and Billy Graham. I am Horace Greeley, Will Rogers, and the Wright brothers. I am George Washington Carver, Daniel Webster, and Jonas Salk.

I am Longfellow, Harriet Beecher Stowe, Walt Whitman, Thomas Paine.

Yes, I am the Nation, and these are the things that I am. I was conceived in freedom, and, God willing, in freedom will I spend the rest of my days. May I possess always the integrity, the courage, and the strength to keep myself unshackled, to remain a citadel of freedom and a beacon of hope to the world.

I am the United States!   — Selected

562. He, who every morning plans the transactions of the day and follows out that plan, carries a thread that will guide him through the labyrinth of the most busy life. The orderly arrangement of his time is like a ray of light which darts itself through all his occupations. But where no plan is laid, where the disposal of time is surrendered merely to the chance of incidents, all things lie huddled together in one chaos, which admits of neither distribution nor review.   — Hugo

563. MAY YOU HAVE
enough happiness to keep you sweet;
enough trials to keep you strong;
enough sorrow to keep you human;
enough hope to keep you happy;
enough failure to keep you humble;
enough success to keep you eager;
enough friends to give you comfort;
enough faith and courage in yourself, your business, and your
    country to banish depression;
enough wealth to meet your needs;
enough determination to make each day a better day than
    yesterday.   —Author Unknown

564. I Am Old Glory
For more than nine score years I have been the banner of hope and freedom for generation after generation of Americans. Born amid the first flames of America's fight for freedom, I am the symbol of a country that has grown from a little group of thirteen colonies to a united nation of fifty sovereign states. Planted firmly on the high pinnacle of American Faith my gently fluttering folds have provided an inspiration to untold millions. Men have followed me into battle with unwavering courage. They have looked upon me as a symbol of national duty. They have prayed that they and their fellow citizens might continue to enjoy the life,

liberty and pursuit of happiness, which have been granted to every American as the heritage of free men. So long as men love liberty more than life itself; so long as they treasure the priceless privileges bought with the blood of our forefathers; so long as the principles of truth, justice and charity for all remain deeply rooted in human hearts, I shall continue to be the enduring banner of the United States of America. *I Am Old Glory!*

— From the *Marine Corps Manual*

565. Liberty lies in the hearts of men and women. When it dies there, no constitution, no law, no court can save it.

— Judge Learned Hand

566. I would rather have a knowledge of the Bible without a college education, than a college education without a knowledge of the Bible. — William Lyons Phelps

567. J. Edgar Hoover has performed a great service in pointing out that Communists are fanatically devoted to their "religion" because they are required to spend much time in studying the original sources of their beliefs, that is, the writings of Marx, Engel and Lenin. All Communists are urged to do this daily and to maintain a schedule of reading throughout youth, in middle life and in old age.

In contrast, Mr. Hoover asks, "Do we as Christians take enough time to read the Bible, and the writings of our prophets, seers and men of God during the past twenty centuries? Are we digging deep enough in the wells of faith?" asks Mr. Hoover. Then he adds, "Most truly, the Bible gives inspiration, zeal and guidance for life. To neglect it is to reduce our national vitality and strength."

Continuing, Mr. Hoover asks a series of questions which every Christian should face and answer: "How many Christians read the Bible only on special occasions? How many Christians set aside a certain amount of time each day or week for reading religious literature? Do some Christians regard the Bible as a book only for children; do they think that as adults they have outgrown it? Do we view the Bible as an 'antique book' which has no message to our modern age? Do we display the same 'iron will and firm determination' to learn the Christian faith as the Communists do for their ideology?"

— *Christian Economics*

568. Q) As a seventeen-year-old high school student what can I do for God? I plan to study for the ministry, but I want to begin to serve Christ now. — P. A.

A) Thank God for your desire to stand up and be counted when so many of our youth have no purpose in life. The depth of your faith in Christ in your teens will reflect the effectiveness of your future ministry.

If I were seventeen and in your position, I would first school myself in the Scriptures. I would read the New Testament, picking out key verses to memorize. David said, "Thy Word have I hid in my heart that I might not sin against Thee." I would make this a major project.

Then, I would seek out other strong Christians in the high school, or community, and get them together into a prayer and discussion group. Seek out ways of winning other students to Christ. Each could invite a non-Christian friend — and they would soon see that you and the other believers had something that they needed. The influence of such a group would be unlimited.

— Billy Graham

569. The following three remarkable comments by college youth were condensed from "The Face of the Future," *Look*, January 12, 1965:

Confessed a 21-year-old college senior: "We mature at the age of 12. We have become world-weary with the boredom of the prostitute who has seen too much of life at the age of sixteen. At 18 we are ready to die.

"We spend our youth chafing in the bonds of the protectivism that smothers and oppresses us. We strike out like little children throwing a tantrum. Our weapons are many: rejection of our parents, the flaunting of our illicit sex lives . . . . The rebellion that seethes in youth today has no foundation. They rebel against what they know not; they are searching for something, but what the something is they cannot say . . . .

"We are the hope of the world, and we have no hope in it. We only have hope in ourselves, and who we are we cannot discover."

Another member of the post-World War II generation, a law student, candidly admits: "What concerns us is a fear of becoming anonymous. We look at the complexity and hugeness of life and wonder how we'll keep our individuality."

From another college senior: "Many of us accept the premises that 'You can't fight City Hall,' 'Live life to its fullest now,' so 'Eat, drink, and make Mary — for tomorrow we will be destroyed by war.'

"I am old-fashioned enough to believe in God, to believe in the dignity and potential of His creation — man, and I'm realistic, not idealistic enough to know that I am not alone in these feelings."

570. Freedom doesn't mean that you can do what you please, but it does mean that there isn't anything holding you back from striving to make your finest dreams come true.

—Wilfred A. Peterson

571. A Communist Party organizer wrote this despairing note to his Kremlin bosses: "It is becoming increasingly difficult to reach downtrodden American masses.

"In the spring, they are forever polishing their shiny new cars.

"In the summer, they take vacations.

"In the fall, they flock to baseball and football games.

"And in the winter, I can't get them to leave their cozy homes and TV sets to hear my lectures.

"How can I make these slaves of capitalism see how oppressed they are?"

572. Ps. 33:12

Two buckets of live crabs, side by side at the fish market, were labeled "$1.50 a dozen," and "$2 a dozen." A patriotic citizen watched them and suddenly a crab from the $1.50 dozen tub climbed up with much effort and dropped into the $2 a dozen tub.

"That's the sort of thing," the patriot told his companion, "which could only happen in America!"

573. Ps. 85:1

The Russian school teacher asked a pupil, "Who were the first human beings?"

"Adam and Eve," the young boy replied.

"What nationality were they?"

"Russian, of course."

"Fine, fine," the teacher commented. "And how did you know they were Russians?"

"Easy," said the boy. "They had no roof over their heads, no clothes to wear, and only one apple for the two of them — and they called it Paradise."

574. Life (James 4:14)

What is life?
Only a whisper,
A fleeting moment
A mist so silently
Unveiled, until
It melts
And disappears,
Lost within the
Multitudes of

Dying Mist.
A piece of clay,
So molded —
A priceless
Work of art —
Or so ruined —
A mass of
Shapeless clay.
A gathering

Of successes	Pathetic dust
Or of failures.	Of deserts;
A light	Carrion —
Whether flickering	The weakness
Or strong;	Of flesh;
Solid as a	Eternal —
Granite cliff;	As a God
Or weak as	Who never dies.

— Donna Balcom, sixteen, *Vision*

575. The Leaden-Eyed

Let not young souls be
　　smothered out before
They do quaint deeds and
　　fully flaunt their pride.
It is the world's one crime
　　its babes grow dull,
Its poor are ox-like, limp
　　and leaden-eyed.
Not that they starve, but
　　starve so dreamlessly;
Not that they sow, but that
　　they seldom reap;
Not that they serve, but
　　have no gods to serve;
Not that they die, but that
　　they die like sheep.

— Vachel Lindsay

576. To love abundantly is to live abundantly, and to love forever is to live forever.

577. Love is the only service that power cannot command, and money cannot buy.

578. I believe that if a man is willing to surrender his will to God he can do anything within the circle of God's will for him.

— John Raley

579. Nothing is really work unless you had rather be doing something else.　　　　　　　　　　　　　　　　　— J. Barrie

580. Government accountants added up a $16,000,000 loss in a single missile development program and attributed it to poor planning and duplication.　　　　　　　　　　June, 1960

581. He Didn't Look Ahead

Construction Digest tells of a young surveyor who was sent out to inspect a section of highway that was frequently flooded. He was told to choose a good site and to erect a warning sign for traffic. He chose a spot close to the lowest part of the road. There he put up a sign which read:

"Notice is hereby given that when this signboard is under water the road is impassable."

582. The cripple who keeps on the way gets to the end of the journey sooner than the runner who goes astray.

583. Activity doesn't necessarily mean achievement. How many are like the cowboy who leaped on his horse and galloped madly in all directions!

584. No wind is favorable if the captain does not know to which port he is steering.

585. B. C. Forbes, American publisher: "Everybody knows that it's bad luck to walk under a ladder. It's worse luck to leap from the bottom round to the top at a single bound. Things that rise rapidly seldom stay up long; every skyrocket has a stick that falls swiftly. Of course, the quicker you can get where you are headed or what you want, the better, but when you get anywhere or anything with little sweat, hold on for dear life. Good things come slowly."

586. A Thought for Today

"A Motto for the Wall"
Who Loves to Soil
His Hands with Toil
Let Him Straightway Go to It!
Myself, I can't Admire the Ant,
And Shall Not Try
To Do It!
I Will Not Drudge!
Indeed, I Grudge
The Time Work Takes — 'Tis Silly!
I Will Not Shirk My Nobler Work
Of Being Just a Lily!
— Don Marquis

587. What the Flag Means to Me

"The flag, to me, stands for freedom and justice. It represents equal opportunity, and gives people a chance to develop their own abilities, to raise their own families, to go to the church of their choice. To put it very simply, the flag points the way to peace, happiness and accomplishment. It does all of this because of what it means to the millions of Americans who believe in the principles it represents and because they are not willing to accept slavery."

— Teresa Stovall, 5th grader of the
Norman Binkley School, Nashville, Tennessee

588. An ambitious young man ventured to approach a great merchant and inquired, "May I ask you the secret of success?"

"There is no secret," replied the merchant. "You just jump at your opportunity." "But how can I tell when my opportunity comes?" "You can't — you have to keep jumping."

589. Opportunity is frequently overlooked because it disguises itself as work.

590. One youngster, asked what he wanted to be when he grew up in this atom age, replied: "Alive."

591. Ability
The winds and the waves are always on the side of the ablest navigators.   — Edward Gibbon

592.   He slept beneath the moon,
He basked beneath the sun,
He lived a life of going-to-do
And died with nothing done.
— James Alberry

593. Father to high-school son: "College — then graduate school —then specialized study! Did your guidance counselor mention anything about a job eventually?"

594. Recently a research organization reported that every day in college was worth $92.59 to the boy or girl concerned.

595. There are three times as many unemployed teen-agers as there are any other classifications of job seekers. About one million seventeen-year-olds entered the labor force this year.

596. Success
Success: Biting off more than you can chew, then chewing it.
Success: An end to be attained not by doing the things we like to do, but by liking the things we have to do.

Success: A thing determined by determination.

Success: Making an ordinary amount of brains do an extraordinary amount of work.

Success: Thoroughly planning your work, then thoroughly working out your plan.

Success: A thing affected not so much by where we stand as by the direction in which we are moving.

Success: A thing which will never come if we are disturbed by the success of others.

Success: A thing half won if we gain the habit of work.

Success: The ability to grasp the main chance when it comes.

Success: That which does not depend so much on sitting up late at night as it does being awake in the daytime.

Success: A ladder we can't climb with our hands in our pockets. — John Garland Pollard

597. Ps. 73:24; Matt. 6:34

Eugene Gilbert, President of the Gilbert Youth Research, Inc., recently concluded a survey in which he asked young people the question, "What is your biggest worry?" The results showed that:

- Nearly twenty-nine per cent said it was concern over the eventual success or failure in life.
- Eighteen per cent felt that their biggest worry was the possibility of school failure.
- Twelve per cent of the boys and girls worried mostly about what young people of their own ages felt about them; that is, the possibility of not being popular.
- After that, on a par on the list of youthful anxieties, were parental disapproval and the state of the world.

It should be noted that the breakdown of the 29 per cent figure worrying about success or failure in life was: 21 per cent for the boys and 36 per cent for the girls. This is a rather surprising figure, since it ordinarily might be assumed that boys would be more concerned with their future than would girls. The possible explanation is that some of the girls felt that success or failure referred principally to marrying and raising a family.

From Mike Kessler, sixteen, of Brooklyn, hopeful of becoming an oceanographer, came the comment that he worried "whether I will leave my mark on the world, or the world will leave its mark on me."

Cliff Collins, seventeen, of Denver, wants to be a success because "being a failure will be letting my parents down." A seventeen-year-old girl, Janet, said eventual success or failure is a worry "because I have not yet defined success and failure for myself. Maybe the greatest success is in pleasing God."

Four per cent of those questioned mentioned certain phobias

and complexes as their main worries in life. Most of those in this category were girls, some of whom were afraid of such things as fish, certain animals and high locations.

598. Things not to Worry About (Heb. 11:6)
Don't worry about popular opinion.
Don't worry about the past.
Don't worry about the future.
Don't worry about growing up.
Don't worry about anybody getting ahead of you.
Don't worry about failures unless it comes through your own fault.
Don't worry about disappointments.
Don't worry about pleasures.
Don't worry about satisfactions.

Something to Think About
What am I really aiming at?
— Taken from a Novelist's letter to his teen-age daughter at camp.

599. Someone has figured out that if a man lives seventy years, twenty will be spent sleeping.
Three years are lost waiting.
Every year thirty hours are lost looking into the mirror.

600. For a More Successful Life (Job 36:11)
1. You will see in others largely what you look for.
2. Don't be a leaner. Your crutch, whatever it may be, will leave you too weak for the task.
3. Failure and success are not accidents or incidents; they are a state of mind.
4. Learn to appreciate God's world. Life will be fascinatingly beautiful if all about you is a revelation of an all-wise Creator.
5. Don't climb the mountain at one leap. If you contemplate such a feat, you will be tired before you start. It is a pleasant ascent when made one step at a time.
6. Always expect something excitingly pleasant just around the corner.
7. Don't be "stymied" by the impossible. The novice is achieving the impossible every day.
8. Never lower yourself to the level of a critic's image of you.
—Herald M. Dozsee

601. When in doubt, speak the truth.

602. "America is great because she is good. If America ever ceases to be good, she will cease to be great."

—Dwight D. Eisenhower

603. It's Your Choice (Rom. 14:12)

If you choose to work, you will succeed; if you don't you will undoubtedly fail.

If you neglect your work, you will dislike it; if you do it well, you will enjoy it.

If you join little cliques, you will be self-satisfied; if you make friends widely, you will interest others.

If you gossip, you will be slandered; if you act like a human being, you will be respected.

If you spurn wisdom, wise people will spurn you; if you seek wisdom, they will seek you.

If you adopt a pose of boredom, you will be a bore; if you show vitality, you will be alive.

If you spend your free time playing bridge, you will be a good bridge player; if you spend it in reading, discussing, and thinking of things that matter, you will become an educated person.

—President Sidney Smith
University of Toronto

Chinese Proverbs (Nos. 604-616)

604. Be forgetful of favors given; be mindful of blessings received.

605. Dig your well before you are thirsty.

606. Heroes walk a dangerous path.

607. Tigers and deer do not stroll together.

608. He who rides a tiger is afraid to dismount.

609. A good horse cannot wear two saddles nor a loyal minister serve two masters.

610. A gem is not polished without rubbing, nor a man perfected without his trials.

611. One wrong thought may cause a life-long regret.

612. Who stands still in mud sticks in it.

613. Laziness in youth means sorrow in old age.

614. Without a smiling face, do not become a merchant.

615. A man's conversation is the mirror of his thoughts.

616. The pleasure of doing good is the only one that will not wear out.

617. An elderly woman told why she is against space travel: "I think people ought to stay home and watch T.V., like the good Lord intended 'em to."

618. Listen Before You Leap (II Chron. 15:5; Ps. 69:20)

Charles Simmons, age seventy-five, tells the story of the nuclear war that destroyed all the cities and all the people of the world, all except, apparently, a lone survivor in Houston. The man walked and walked and walked, desolate and despairing, through the rubbled city, through the destroyed countryside, and on to Galveston.

At last he decided to return to Houston, where he found no human, no animal of any kind. Yet somehow one skyscraper still stood, largely intact. And so the last human being began climbing the stairs to the top of the sixty-story building. As he now viewed the destruction of his city from his aerial perch, he was overcome. He decided to join the millions of departed souls.

He stepped out on the ledge of the sixtieth floor and jumped — and just at that instant the telephone in the office rang.

619. Stay on the Job (Luke 19:12-27)

A king of England once visited a certain hotel. The news got around; people stopped working and gathered around the hotel hoping to see the king. But the king stepped unobserved out of a back way through the garden. In the field beyond, a woman was tending her plants. The king asked, "Where is your master?" "Gone to see the king," she replied, "with all the rest of the workmen." The king handed her a coin and said, "Tell them you have seen the king because you 'stayed on the job'." She was occupied when the king came. May our Lord so find us when He comes!

620. What Is Your Mission? (Job 12:25; Prov. 4:26; John 18:37)

Dr. R. W. Sockman says that a company of college students were asked, "What is your mission in life?" There was a painful silence. Finally, one spoke up and said, "I guess it's to get ahead in the world, isn't it?"

The questioner went on to say that he reported the incident to a company of business men and they could not see much wrong with the answer.

If the only mission we can set before our young people and ourselves is just to get ahead in the world, meaning thereby to get a larger salary and have a finer house, then we may keep up with the Joneses, but we will not keep up with the Khrushchevs. America will lose out in the race with other nations and, what is more, she will lose her own soul.

621.

A Psalm of Life

Lives of great men all remind us
We can make our lives sublime,
And, departing, leave behind us
Footprints on the sands of time.

Let us then be up and doing,
With a heart for any fate;
Still achieving, still pursuing,
Learn to labor and to wait.

—Longfellow

622. He who wishes to fulfill his mission in the world must be a man of one idea that is one of the great overmastering purposes, overshadowing all his aims, and guiding and controlling his entire life.

—Bates

623. The Winning (Job 28:13; Ps. 17:3)

What if you came out second
In the race that you have run?
If you put your best in running,
In the final score, you won!
If you kept the goal before you,
And played the game, I'd 'low,
E'en though another took the prize —
You won it anyhow!

You won the greater battle
When you played it fair and right;
Although another touched the goals,
You really won the fight.
Just keep your standard flying,
And don't give up the game;
The second place, with honor,
Beats any first, with shame.

—Anonymous

624. Give the future prayerful consideration; that's where you'll spend the rest of your life.

625. Superior Leadership (Hag. 2:23; Acts 9:15)

Leadership is ahead for you. Your ability to lead will be gained through training, study, through living and working together with others. Your school provides you with optimum opportunities to learn and train for leadership. I challenge you to be a *leader.*

Excellence is required if you are to lead. You can excel in one or more ways. By striving for this excellence, you are preparing for your career. Be your best, and do your best. I challenge you to be *excellent.*

Thoroughness characterizes you as a leader. Leave nothing to chance or luck. Discipline yourself. Give yourself to minute details. Follow instructions carefully. Neglect of details will cheat you of the future rewards of industriousness and advancement in leadership. I challenge you to be *thorough.*

Promptness is your habit if you are to be a leader. As a leader you will keep a schedule. In so-called unimportant matters, the habit of promptness will be developed so that when important opportunities come, the characteristic of being prompt will reward you. Tardiness will rob you of the rewards of ambition and effort. I challenge you to be *prompt.*

Neatness helps a leader. Your attire, your affairs, your work are enhanced by neatness. Everything about you indicates the kind of person you are. Strive then for neatness. It is an index of your future as a leader. I challenge you to be *neat.*

Obedience is your best key to leadership. If you would lead, learn to obey. Your school is a good place in which to train your mind and spirit into a life-habit of obedience. Of all the lessons to be learned, this is one of the greatest. If you learn to obey, you will have learned to command. I challenge you to *obedience.*
—J. Robert Ashcroft

626. Matt. 20:26, 27

The reason why rivers and seas receive the homage of a hundred mountain streams is that they keep below them. Thus they are able to reign over all the mountain streams. So the sage, wishing to be above men, putteth himself below them; wishing to be before them, he putteth himself behind them. Thus, though his place be above men, they do not feel his weight; though his place be before them, they do not count it an injury.

—Lao Tsze, Chinese sage of twenty-five centuries ago

627. Matt. 9:29; Luke 17:5

> Satisfy your want and wish power by
> overcoming your can't and won't power
> with can and will power.
>
> —Wm. J. H. Boetcher

628. When it is definitely settled that a thing can't be done, watch someone do it.

Nothing turns out right unless someone makes it his job to see that it does.

"Attempt great things for God; expect great things from God."
—William Carey

629.
> All that stands between your goal
> And the deeds you hope to do,
> And the dreams which stir your restless soul —
> Is you!

630.
> The way is rough and the way is long,
> And the end is hid from view,
> But the one to say if you shall be strong —
> Is you!
>
> —Anonymous

631. The dictionary is the only place where success comes before work.

632. Choice
> To every man there openeth
> A Way, and Ways, and a Way,
> And the High Soul climbs the High Way,
> And the Low Soul gropes the Low,
> And in between, on the misty flats,
> The rest drift to and fro.
> But to every man there openeth
> A High Way and a Low.
> And every man decideth
> The Way his soul shall go.
>
> —John Oxenham

633. Success has a way of coming in a hurry after you have endured a long haul of plodding along slowly.

634.
> Only one life, 'twill soon be past;
> Only what's done for Christ will last.
>
> —Unknown

635. A Big Man is not one who makes no mistakes, but one who is bigger than any mistake he makes.

636.   What we are is God's gift to us.
               What we become is our gift to God.
                                        —Louis Nizer

637. Test Case (I Cor. 1:26; II Peter 1:10)
The following story going the rounds appeared in *The Financial Post*, Canada, and has a moral for test-happy executives who rely on complicated, expensive tests in hiring employees:

A firm needed a researcher. Applicants were a scientist, an engineer, an economist. Each was given a stone, a piece of string, a stop watch — and told to determine a certain building's height. The scientist went to the rooftop, tied the stone to the string, lowered it to the ground. Then he swung it, timing each swing with the watch. With this pendulum he estimated the height at two hundred feet, give or take twelve inches. . . . The engineer threw away the string, dropped the stone from the roof, timing its fall with the watch. Applying the laws of gravity, he estimated the height at two hundred feet, give or take six inches. . . . The economist, ignoring string and stone, entered the building but soon returned to report the height at exactly two hundred feet. How did he know? He gave the janitor the watch in exchange for the building plans. He got the job.

638. Our nation was founded by overcoming adversity. From the time of the early patriots — the pioneers, the Civil War, World War I, the great depression of the 1930's and World War II — there has always been a challenge for us to meet and conquer. Greatness won, though the challenge of adversity can be lost through inaction and lethargy.

Our challenge lies directly before us. The course is indelibly clear. Ours is a just cause. If we have faith in humanity, if we seek God's divine guidance, if we summon the courage of our fore-fathers, our heritage of freedom will be preserved.

History teaches us that we must carefully tend the fires of freedom here at home — for the light of free men will penetrate the darkness of tyranny wherever it exists in the world, bringing home and trust in our noble cause.

We must dedicate ourselves to the principle that freedom under God is man's destiny. We must not only live our lives according to this principle but also defend it unto death with the courage of free men.

Let us live our lives so that we may proclaim to the whole world:

"Individual freedom is our creed — national freedom is our heritage — world freedom is our goal."

—From an address by J. Edgar Hoover
"The Courage of Free Men"

639. Jonah 1:8; I Cor. 7:17; Eph. 4:11

Three young boys were bragging about their dads.

"My dad writes a couple of lines," the first boy said, "calls it a poem and gets $10 for it."

"My dad makes dots on paper, calls it a song," the second said, "and gets $25 for it."

"That's nothing," said the third boy. "My dad writes a sermon on a sheet of paper, gets up in the pulpit and reads it and it takes four men to bring the money in."

640. Any weakling can be a peace-breaker; only the strong can be a peace-maker.

641. Every right implies a responsibility; every opportunity, an obligation; every possession, a duty.

642. It takes nature ten years to grow an oak; six months to grow a squash.

643. When you make your mark in the world, watch out for guys with erasers.

644. You can tell that many of us believe that today's greatest labor-saving device is tomorrow.

645. A Mere Slip of the Pen (I Peter 3:15)

With a rather pleasant blend of apprehension and anticipation, Miss Fran Doolan of Houston, Texas, is expecting to hear from her draft board almost any day now.

She doesn't know whether the board will send a detachment of soldiers for her, or merely write a letter, but she knows the question that will be asked: "Why didn't you register for the draft, as the law requires, on your eighteenth birthday last November?"

Let's get it straight now. Miss Doolan is not a draft-dodger.

But some confusion is likely to arise from the fact that her birth certificate has her listed as "male" — a slight error which was made eighteen years ago, but discovered only the other day when Miss Doolan and a friend happened to be examining the certificate.

Many an eighteen-year-old will wish he had as good an answer to that why-didn't-you-register question as Miss Doolan has.
—Allison Sanders, *The Houston Chronicle*

646. The Moving Finger writes; and, having writ,
Moves on: nor all your Piety nor Wit
Shall lure it back to cancel half a Line,
Nor all your Tears wash out a Word of it.
—Omar Khayyam

647. Four things a man must learn to do
If he would make his calling true:
To think without confusion clearly,
To love his fellow men sincerely,
To act from honest motives purely,
To trust in God and heaven securely.
—Henry Van Dyke

SUBJECT INDEX

Subjects are indexed by number of entry, not by page.

Ability, 533, 592
Achievement, 627-630, 634, 636
Action, 55
Activity, 583
Adaptability, 364
Adolescence, 26, 38, 104, 132
  Awkwardness of, 23, 177
  Biological development of, 327
  Characteristics of, 53
  Misunderstood, 1
Adult, 28
Adversity, 638
Age, 25
Aim, 268
Alcohol, 6, 491, 529
Alibi, 218
Allowance, 116, 376
Alternative, 397, 522
Ambition, 590
America, 602
Ancestry, 138, 171
Appreciation, 153
Appetite, 74, 75
Aptitude, 557
Arguing, 122
Assistance, 334
Athletics, 401
Attemptability, 548
Attendance, Church, 488
Attention, 252
Attitude, 83, 96, 97, 100, 286, 347, 348
Automobile, 24, 130, 133, 146, 180, 196, 197

Babysitter, 134
Balance, 563
Beauty, 17, 350
Beginning, 199
Beliefs, 549
Bible, 237, 395, 485, 509, 566, 567
Blood, Christ's, 508
Boast, 254, 380, 486
Boy, 201
British Teens, 88
Broadmindedness, 435

Calling, 647
Candy, 164
Capitalism, 571
Character, 81, 82, 89, 178, 188, 194, 402, 449

Cheating, 214, 248
Choice, 445, 603, 632
Christianity, 470
Cigarettes, 7, 9
  Smoking and grades, 8
Clothes, 390, 391, 397
College, Entrance requirements of, 265
Communism, 567
Communistic Theory
  Impracticality of, 233
Compensation, 436
Concealment, 84
Concentration, 243
Conduct, Church, 524
Confidence, 32
Conformity, 575
Conscience, 447, 536
Consecration, 535, 578
Consequences, 454, 457, 608
Contentment, 54
Convalescence, 43
Conviction, 448, 549
Cosmetics, 337
Cowardice, 525
Crime, 501
Criticism, 331, 359, 461, 464

Decency in standard of dress, 478-480
Deception, 518
Decision, 47, 531
Dedication, 42
Degree, Worth of college, 210
Democracy, 556
Devil, 512
Dieting, 34
Dilemma, 188
Diploma, 205
Diplomacy, 355, 404
Direction, 103
Disagreements, 362
Disappointment, 410
Discipline, 131, 159, 160, 198, 226
Discovery, 147
Discretion, 389, 439
Disposition, 36
Divorce, 142
Dollars, Value of, 182
Draft, Exempt from, 645
Dropouts
  Church, 541
  School, 207, 236, 256, 275, 277

Dual Nature, 456
Dutch Proverbs, 91-93

Economics, 117-119
Education, 203, 282, 289, 294-306
    and Spirituality, 284
    Monetary value of, 208, 221, 288,
        594
Egotism, 370, 379, 387, 426, 427, 438
Embarrassment, 433
Enemies, 342, 343, 369, 398, 607
English, 251
Environment, 125, 169
Escape, 258
Evaluation, 356, 421
Evolution, 11, 505
Example, 170, 248, 310, 354, 465, 489,
    621
Excess, 191, 377, 434
Excuse, 263
Exercise, 48
Experience, 31, 102
Extremes, 91, 206

Failure, 71-73, 229, 230, 285, 286
Faithfulness, 582, 619, 623
Family
    Altar, 190
    Definition of, 140
    Fact about, 174
    Worth of, 155
Family Tree, 129
Father, 143, 148, 149, 157, 167, 168,
    173, 183, 500
Fear, 540
Fight, 60
Flag, U.S., 564, 587
Food, Cost of, 163
Forgiveness, 444
Freedom, 570
Friend, 345, 346, 368
    Definition of, 320, 340
Friends, Difference between, 415
Friendship, 315-319, 341
Frustrations of college youth, 61, 428
Futility, 58, 87, 172, 211, 510
Future, 624
    Attitudes toward, 569

Genius, 307
Gethsemane, 466
Gift, Pentecostal, 523
Glossary of Teen Terms, 313
Goal, 584
Gossip, 467
Grades, 238

Graduates, High School, 209
Gratitude, 495, 604
Group Opinion, 407, 408
Guilt, 511

Habit, 450
Hair, 18
Handicaps, 384
Happiness, 37, 416
Health, 46
Height, 19, 20
Hell, 502
Helplessness, 472
History, 246, 247, 560
Home, 106-115, 175, 178
Honesty, 213, 262
Honor, 69
Honor Roll, 267
Household Ills, 187
Humiliation, 312
Humility, 498
Hyper-sensitivity, 394

Immaturity, 76, 101
Immorality, 551
Immortality, 506
Imperceptibility, 330
Improvement, 80
Impossibilities, 458, 538, 546
Impression, 181
Identity, 383
Income, Teen, 40, 328
Indecision, 396
Indifference
    Mental, 575
    Spiritual, 490
Indispensable, 12, 24
Individual, Importance of, 274
Inferiority Complex, 335
Influence, 120, 121, 344, 516, 517,
    532
Ingenuity, 244, 249, 292, 637
Initiative, 72, 92, 278, 323
Insight, 239, 245
Interpretation, 124
Inventors, Teen, 52

Jail, 175
Jesus Christ, 20, 453, 522, 553, 554
Juvenile Deliquency, 105
    Predictability of, 552

Kiss, 215
Knowledge, 240, 260, 270

Law, Divorce, 371
Leadership, 625, 626

Lecture, 253
Liberty, 565
Life, 39, 70, 150, 193, 507, 539, 574, 576
Literature
  Effects of, 216, 459
  Realism in, 217
Love, 330, 374
  God's, 500, 577
Loyalty, 609

Man, 49, 50
Manners, 430
Marriage, 374, 375, 392, 393
Mathematics, 229, 290
Maturity, 154, 361, 641
Mental Health, 15
Middle Age, 27
Mind, Singleness of, 622
Ministry, 293
  Limitations of, 460
  Planning for, 568
Miscalculation, 219
Missionary, 249, 484
Missions, 514
Mistakes, 372
Misunderstanding, 409, 440, 455
Money, 30, 222
  and Ministry, 639
Mother
  Confide in, 184
  Honor of, 141
  Roles of, 189

Naivete, 411
Narrowmindedness, 354
Nationality, 422
Newlyweds, 158
Nonsense Poems, 4
Nutrition, 21, 51, 74

Obstacle, 273, 606, 635
Obstetrician, 139
Openmindedness, 269
Opportunism, 81
Opportunity, 388, 451, 519-521, 588, 589
Orchid, 376
Order, 181, 231
Originality, 283
Overcoming, 59, 60, 85, 127, 162, 612

Parents
  Admiration for, 176
  Advice of, 123
  Love for, 136
  Respect for, 126

Parenthood, Teen Thoughts on, 189
Past, The, 646
Patriotism, 559, 572
Peace, 185, 186, 640
Pearl, 137
Pentecost, 442, 523
Perplexity, 231
Perseverance, 202
Personality, 321
Personal Worth, 77
  Teen definition of, 192
Petition, 255
Petting, 420
Physique, 4
Physical Development
  Glandular function, 5
Physical Fitness, 44, 95
Plan, 562
Planning, 580, 581
Pleasure, 616
Politics, 287
Popularity, 314, 322, 326, 338, 339, 347, 349, 351, 358, 360, 365, 381, 406
Population, 3
  Increase in teens, 2
Possession, 546
Praise, 399
Preparation, 280, 291, 293, 605
Presumption, 411, 618
Pride, 545
Procrastination, 223
Professors, 309
Promotion, 212
Prudence, 195
Psychology, 395
Punctuation, 281
Purpose, Life's, 620

Qualifications, 515
Quarreling, Effects of, 162
Questions, 234

Rationalization, 413
Recognition, 264, 423
Report cards, 166, 261
Reputation, 332, 333, 373, 402, 468
Resentment, 386
Respect, 432
Response, 544
Responsibility, 67, 68, 200, 558
Results, 235
Righteousness, 185
Romance, 336, 384

Salvation, 463

Sarcasm, 357
Shock, 308
School, 279
Science and Religion, 504
Self-mastery, 481
Self-sufficiency, 462
Self-respect, 487
Serenity, 475, 530
Sermons, Dry, 493
Sex, Weaker, 353
  Unrestricted, 452
Share, 324
Siblings, 145, 151
Silence, 272
Sin, 497, 527, 550
Sincerity, 547
Sluggard, 586, 592, 613
Smile, 403, 614
Social Growth, affected by biological functions, 327
Son, Ungrateful, 179
Soul, Satisfaction for the, 441
Sowing and Reaping, 471
Space, 262
Statistics, Ratio of age to Converson, 513
Status Symbol, 494
Strength, 477
Study, 204, 205, 232
Success, 242, 276, 557, 596, 600, 631, 643
Suggestion, Power of, 384
Suicide, 35, 400
Symbolism in romance, 220

Teen-age buying and spending, 62-66
Teen-ager, An open letter to, 156
Teen Commandments, 56
Teen Slang, 94
Telephone, 154, 378, 382
Television, 241, 617

Temper, 363
Temptation, 446, 451, 469, 499, 534
Tests, 637
Thought, 611, 615
Thoughtfulness, 312
Time, 90, 98, 99, 585, 599, 633
Today, 551
Tomorrow, 644
Translation of parent talk, 135
Trend, Modern, 227, 250, 252, 378
Trials, 610
Trouble, 93, 325, 385, 543
Truth, 542, 601

Understanding, 431, 482
Unhappiness, 57, 528
United States, The, 561
Unemployment in teens, 595
Unselfishness, 141
Usefulness, 16

Values, 45, 445
Venereal Disease, 10, 419
Verification, 254
Virtues, 367
Vocabulary, 281

Waste, 275, 311
Weakness, 266, 537
Weight, 413
Wisdom, 228, 492
Wit, 228
Witnessing, 443
Wolf, 425
Wonder, 225
Word Labels, 417, 418
Words, 259, 267
  Needed at home, 144
Work, 41, 380, 579, 593
World, 483, 597, 598

Youth, 329, 526, 527
Youthfulness, 22, 29

INDEX OF NAMES

Names are indexed by number of entry, not by page.

Adams, Darrel, 500
Adams, James T., 302
Adams, John, 127
Addison, 299
Adolfson, L. H., 203
Aesop, 169
Alberry, James, 592
Allen, Charles L. 106, 314, 323, 499
Allen, Roger, 36
Alvarez, Walter C., 15
Anderson, Alexander, 52
Aristotle, 295
Ashcroft, Robert J., 625
Augustine, 527
Ayer, W. W., 108

Balcom, Donna 574
Barnardo, 463
Barrie, J., 579
Bates, 622
Baylor, C. H., 528
Beecher, Henry W., 517
Bennett, Leo, 547
Berry, Melinda P., 478
Billings, Josh, 385
Boetcher, Wm. J. H., 627
Bowman, Nancy, 134
Brooks, Phillips, 314
Brown, William J., 419
Buchanan, James, 127
Buckhorn, Robert, 21

Caldwell, Louis O., 53, 54, 155, 222, 358, 524, 533
Camus, Albert, 216
Carey, William, 169, 628
Carver, George W., 561
Chapman, J. Wilbur, 535
Chappell, Clovis, 445
Chesterfield, 360, 437
Churchill, Winston, 261
Cicero, 433
Clark, Blake
Cleveland, Grover, 127
Compton, Arthur H., 504
Cone, Thomas E., 327
Conklin, Edwin, 505
Corman, Rena, 61
Cowper, William, 316
Crane, Frank, 340
Criswold, Whitney A., 487
Crockett, Davy, 561

Darwin, Charles, 261
Delaney, Walt, 420
Demke, Barbara 132
Donne, John, 462
Dozsee, Herald M., 600
Dreier, Thomas, 270
Dulaney, Ele, 420

Edison, Thomas A., 52, 261, 286, 561
Edwards, Jonathan, 19
Einstein, Albert, 266, 507, 561
Eisenhower, Dwight D., 601
Eliot, George, 261
Engel, 567
Ericson, Gayle, 150, 453
Evans, Elizabeth, 556

Fillmore, Millard, 127
Flynn, Clarence E., 228
Forbes, B. C., 585
Ford, Henry, 71
Ford, Sharon, 69
Foster, Steven, 561
Franklin, Benjamin, 373, 377, 379, 561
Frost, Robert, 195
Fuller, Margaret, 70
Fuller, Thomas, 341
Furguson, 169

Galileo, 52, 290
Galton, Lawrence, 210
Gansaulas, 443
Garfield, James A., 127
Gay, John, 317
Getty, J. Paul, 30
Gibbon, Edward, 519
Giblin, Les, 395
Gilbert, Eugene, 597
Glick, Paul C., 208
Glueck, Eleanor T., 552
Glueck, Sheldon, 552
Graham, Billy, Int., 162, 452, 561, 568
Gran, John M., 1, 226
Grant, Ulysses, 127, 561
Greeley, Horace, 561
Guest, Edgar A., 536
Guinn, Jack, 30

Hale, Edward E., 55
Hale, Nathan, 561
Hand, L., 565
Harmodius, 138
Harral, Stewart, 309

Haskin, Dorothy C., 513
Hazlitt, William, 342
Heald, Henry T., 282
Heard, R. D., 549
Henry, Matthew, 526
Henry, Patrick, 561
Hilton, Conrad, 274
Hollandsworth, Luke, 548
Hoover, J. Edgar, 105, 186, 567, 638
Hope, Galen, 259
Horn, Trader, 301
Hoyt, K. B., 236
Hugo, Victor, 562
Hunt, Morton M., 61
Huxley, 298

Iphicrates, 138

Jackson, Andrew, 127
James, William, 465
Jefferson, Thomas, 561
Johnson, Andrew, 127
Johnson, Lady Bird, 236
Johnson, Luci, 128
Johnson, Samuel, 315, 450
Jones, Bob, 520
Jones, E. Stanley, 522
Jones, John P., 561
Jonson, Ben, 485

Keller, Father, 480, 539
Khayyam, Omar, 646
Kilander, Fredrick H., 186
Kirkendall, Lester A., 167
Klapp, Orrin, 250
Kreisler, Fritz, 495

La Frochefoucauld, 318
Landers, Ann, 168
Landsdowne, Paul, 501
Lasky, Jerome M., 418
Lee, Robert E., 561
Lenin, Nikolai, 567
Lewis, Audree, 450
Lewis, George H., 98
Lichter, Solomon, 536
Lincoln, Abraham, 127, 169, 194, 280, 285, 322, 386, 477, 561
Linsay Vachel, 575
Longfellow, Henry W., 170, 561, 621
Lopez, Alejandro, 216
Lowe, Juliette, 329
Lowell, James R., 261
Lund, Marshall, 43
Luther, Martin, 169, 483

McCormick, Cyrus Hall, 52
McKenzie, 405, 432
McKinley, William, 127
McMillan, Jerry, 244
Maclaren, Alexander, 515
Madden, Eileen, 124
Madison, James, 19
Maerz, Cindy, 260
Makwa, L. L., 175
Malloch, Douglas, 115
Manley, Grandy, Int.
Mann, Horace, 296
Marshall, Peter, 508
Martin, J. B., 175
Marting, Stephanic, 73
Marquis, Dr., 586
Marx, Karl, 567
Maxwell, Edward L., 419
Metcalfe, James J., 123
Michelangelo, 242
Miller, Anne Bell, 352
Miller, Fred, 502
Miller, Leonard, 111
Miller, Pauline, 111
Miller, Ruth, 421
Modell, Leonole, 42
Moliere, 273
Molner, Joseph, 6
Moody, Dwight L., 442
Moore, Martha, 61
Moore, Woodvall, 541
Myer, F. B., 523

Napoleon, 261
Nelson, Esther Marion, Int.
Newton, Isaac, 261
Nizer, Louis, 636

Oxenham, John, 632

Paine, Thomas, 561
Parkhurst, Charles H., 449
Patterson, Alec, 481
Penn, William, 482
Pericles, 559
Peterson, Wilfred A., 326, 570
Phelps, William L., 321, 566
Plato, 467
Platt, Prudence, 306
Plautus, 346
Polk, James K., 127
Pollard, John, 6, 596
Pope, Alexander, 297
Porterfield, Bruce E., 249
Powell, H. F., 529
Price, John E., 113
Pumroy, Donald, 7

Raley, John, 578
Revere, Paul, 561
Robertson, James H., 61
Rogers, Will, 561
Rosanfield, Emanuel, 149
Ross, Betsy, 561
Royko, Mile, 264
Ruskin, 300, 557
Ruth, Babe, 561
Ryan, Frank, 219

Sainsbury, Allison, 188
Salber, Eva
Salk, Jonas, 561
Salinger, J. D., 217
Sandburg, Carl, 556
Sanders, Allison, 645
Santayana, 246
Schreiber, Daniel, 236
Schwartz, William F., 10
Scott, Walter, 518
Scovel, S. F., 303
Seneca, 345
Shakespeare, William, 343, 485
Shearer, Lloyd, 96
Simmons, Charles, 618
Skrycki, Carol, 292
Smith, Homer, 479
Smith, Sidney, 603
Sockman, R. W., 620
Spindler, Evelyn, 21
Spurgeon, Charles H., Int., 19
Stacks, Clyde, 175
Stacks, Lucille, 175

Stallings, Gene, 448
Stanley, Bob, 310
Stevenson, Adlai, 438
Stevenson, Robert L., 202
Steward, James S., Int.
Stovall, Teresa, 587
Stowe, Harriet B., 561
Summers, Phil, 244
Swope, Herbert B., 72

Tagg, Leonard, 287
Terry, Luther, 419
Trowbridge, J. T., 344
Tsze, Lao, 626
Twain, Mark, 84, 283, 311
Tyson, Robert, 218

Van Buren, Abby, 160, 161
Van Doren, Mark, 243
Van Dyke, Henry, 647
Von Braun, Magnue, 229
Von Braun, Wernher, 229, 506

Washington, Burnette, 236
Washington, George, 319, 561
Watt, James, 52, 561
Webster, Daniel, 304, 509, 561
Welch, Wayne, 216
Westinghouse, George, 52
Whitman, Walt, 561
Whitney, Eli, 561
Wilson, Thomas, 339
Wright, Wilbur, 561

Zuck, Roy, B., 541

INDEX OF SCRIPTURAL REFERENCES

Names are indexed by number of entry, not by page.

GENESIS
1:26, 27 — 46
11:4 — 314
11:7 — 234
41:39 — 384

EXODUS
20:12 — 126

NUMBERS
1:8 — 11
13 — 219
14:1-25 — 219

DEUTERONOMY
1:41 — 293
12:30 — 216
20:8 — 516
24:16 — 138
29:29 — 460

JUDGES
12:6 — 251
16:4-21 — 364
16:17 — 18
17:6 — 452

I SAMUEL
9:27 — 203
9:32 — 327
18:1 — 368
26:21 — 420

II SAMUEL
10:12 — 556
18:3 — 533
18:5 — 548
19:35 — 287
20:9 — 21

I KINGS
3:12 — 250
11:28 — 202
21:7 — 403

II CHRONICLES
15:5 — 618

ESTHER
3:1-6 — 57
4:14 — 443

JOB
2:3 — 266
12:25 — 623
19:4 — 457
23:8 — 229
28:13 — 276
28:16 — 45
32:18 — 357

32:21 — 417
36:11 — 600
37:21 — 96

PSALMS
1:2 — 203
4:6 — 347
16:6 — 11
17:3 — 623
17:5 — 1
19:10 — 40
19:12 — 2, 281
19:14 — 313, 381
31:3 — 103
33:1 — 399
33:12 — 556, 572
34:4 — 428
40:12 — 18
40:17 — 462
42:11 — 15
69:20 — 618
71:1 — 104, 234
73:24 — 597
74:16 — 43
85:1 — 573
90:12 — 135, 421
90:17 — 17
100:3 — 5
101:2 — 524
118:24 — 555
119:45 — 397
122:6 — 378
133:1 — 106

PROVERBS
1:4 — 498
1:8 — 123
3:7 — 387
3:21, 23 — 288
4:7, 8 — 1
4:7 — 355
5:15 — 106
5:22 — 489
11:25 — 349
12:2 — 478
12:15 — 51, 56
13:5 — 478
13:24 — 197
14:9 — 550
15:1 — 362
15:5 — 195
15:23 — 144
17:1 — 106

17:17 — 368
20:1 — 491
22:1 — 322, 417
22:3 — 195
23:29, 30 — 6
26:27 — 489
27:14 — 496
28:10 — 40
29:11 — 228
29:16 — 538
30:13 — 387
31:10, 30 — 478

ECCLESIASTES
2:13 — 420
5:12 — 30
7:8 — 229
7:25 — 504
9:18 — 249
11:6 — 306

ISAIAH
1:18 — 56
5:12 — 4
6:8 — 533
11:2, 3 — 135
16:7 — 19
20:18 — 473
24:9 — 6
26:21 — 51
28:10 — 306
52:7 — 17
58:12 — 444
59:2 — 550
64:6 — 463
65:5 — 387
65:22 — 347

JEREMIAH
2:32 — 383
15:18 — 61
32:33 — 207
48:41 — 244

EZEKIEL
7:23 — 551

DANIEL
1:4 — 292, 504

HOSEA
10:13 — 419
13:6 — 125
14:9 — 384

JONAH
1:8 — 639

MICAH
6:7 _____ 10
13:13 _____ 538

HAGGAI
2:23 _____ 625

MATTHEW
6:8 _____ 463
6:21 _____ 378
6:34 _____ 43, 597
7:11 _____ 124
9:6 _____ 444
9:29 _____ 627
10:30 _____ 18
12:34 _____ 458
13:14 _____ 354
15:19, 20 _____ 551
15:19 _____ 217
19:6 _____ 371
20:26, 27 _____ 626
24:14 _____ 514
25:46 _____ 502

MARK
14:70 _____ 313
16:15 _____ 514

LUKE
2:20 _____ 53
2:40 _____ 327
2:51 _____ 105, 126
5:26 _____ 4
6:24 _____ 30
12:33 _____ 30, 421
14:11 _____ 381
14:18 _____ 218
17:5 _____ 627
19:20 _____ 463
19:12-23 _____ 619

JOHN
2:1, 2 _____ 392
3:16 _____ 500
4:7-29 _____ 441
5:44 _____ 323
6:63 _____ 528
8:9 _____ 536
9:24 _____ 443
10:10 _____ 475
10:27 _____ 103

ACTS
2:33 _____ 321
3:6 _____ 52
4:3 _____ 532
4:12 _____ 321, 522
7:30-32, 34 _____ 293
9:15 _____ 625
21:37 _____ 306
24:16 _____ 242

ROMANS
2:9 _____ 61
12:1 _____ 7, 42, 495
12:10 _____ 349
13:14 _____ 452
14:7 _____ 516
14:12 _____ 603
14:13 _____ 489
14:14-23 _____ 445
15:2 _____ 306
16:18 _____ 51

I CORINTHIANS
1:26 _____ 637
2:3 _____ 428
3:17 _____ 420
3:18 _____ 228
4:1 _____ 323
4:7 _____ 461
7:7 _____ 52
7:17 _____ 639
7:35 _____ 243
8:2 _____ 228
8:9 _____ 397
9:22 _____ 364
9:24 _____ 323
10:6 _____ 216
10:13 _____ 499
11:20-23 _____ 42
13:9 _____ 460
14:19 _____ 267
14:20 _____ 464
15:3 _____ 42

II CORINTHIANS
1:6 _____ 355
6:14, 17 _____ 374
8:11 _____ 401

GALATIANS
5:13 _____ 452
6:7 _____ 10, 233
6:9 _____ 202, 458
6:10 _____ 287

EPHESIANS
2:10 _____ 5
4:11 _____ 639
5:18 _____ 6, 491
5:20 _____ 495

PHILIPPIANS
2:4 _____ 156
2:5 _____ 528
3:7 _____ 45, 276
4:8 _____ 347, 494
4:11 _____ 473
4:13 _____ 127
4:19 _____ 463

COLOSSIANS
4:6 _____ 313, 381

I THESSALONIANS
4:10 _____ 327
4:11 _____ 203
5:21 _____ 538

II THESSALONIANS
3:7 _____ 524

I TIMOTHY
1:5 _____ 536
2:8, 9 _____ 383
2:9 _____ 479
4:7 _____ 401
4:8 _____ 265
4:12 _____ 352, 516

II TIMOTHY
1:7 _____ 428
2:15 _____ 204
2:21 _____ 533
2:22 _____ 452
3:1, 2 _____ 217

TITUS
1:15 _____ 550
2:4, 5 _____ 384
3:9 _____ 11

HEBREWS
10:35 _____ 219
11:6 _____ 598
11:25 _____ 419
12:1 _____ 7, 445

JAMES
1:4 _____ 473
1:12 _____ 499
2:22 _____ 548
3:23 _____ 417
4:3 _____ 457
4:14 _____ 574
5:11 _____ 43
5:16 _____ 266

I PETER
2:6 _____ 234
3:3, 4 _____ 479
3:4 _____ 17
3:8 _____ 464
3:15 _____ 271, 645
3:16 _____ 281
4:10 _____ 124
5:12 _____ 357

II PETER
1:10 _____ 637

III JOHN
1:2 _____ 46

149

DATE DUE